1986

University of St. Francis

D1366241

Increasing the Use of Institutional Research

Jack Lindquist, *Editor*

NEW DIRECTIONS FOR INSTITUTIONAL RESEARCH

Sponsored by the Association for Institutional Research

MARVIN W. PETERSON, *Editor-in-Chief*

Number 32, December 1981

Paperback sourcebooks in
The Jossey-Bass Higher Education Series

Jossey-Bass Inc., Publishers
San Francisco • Washington • London

LIBRARY
College of St. Francis
JOLIET, ILL.

Increasing the Use of Institutional Research
Volume VIII, Number 4, December 1981
     Jack Lindquist, *Editor*

New Directions for Institutional Research Series
Marvin W. Peterson, *Editor-in-Chief*

Copyright © 1981 by Jossey-Bass Inc., Publishers
                            and
                    Jossey-Bass Limited

Copyright under International, Pan American, and Universal
Copyright Conventions. All rights reserved. No part of
this issue may be reproduced in any form — except for brief
quotation (not to exceed 500 words) in a review or professional
work — without permission in writing from the publishers.

New Directions for Institutional Research (publication number
USPS 098-830) is published quarterly by Jossey-Bass Inc.,
Publishers, and is sponsored by the Association for Institutional
Research. The volume and issue numbers above are included for
the convenience of libraries. Second-class postage rates paid at
San Francisco, California, and at additional mailing offices.

Correspondence:
Subscriptions, single-issue orders, change of address notices,
undelivered copies, and other correspondence should be sent to
New Directions Subscriptions, Jossey-Bass Inc., Publishers,
433 California Street, San Francisco, California 94104.

Editorial correspondence should be sent to the Editor-in-Chief,
Marvin W. Peterson, Center for the Study of Higher Education,
University of Michigan, Ann Arbor, Michigan 48109.

Library of Congress Catalogue Card Number LC 80-84287
International Standard Serial Number ISSN 0271-0579
International Standard Book Number ISBN 87589-844-0

Cover art by Willi Baum
Manufactured in the United States of America

378.0072
L748

Ordering Information

The paperback sourcebooks listed below are published quarterly and can be ordered either by subscription or as single copies.

Subscriptions cost $30.00 per year for institutions, agencies, and libraries. Individuals can subscribe at the special rate of $18.00 per year *if payment is by personal check*. (Note that the full rate of $30.00 applies if payment is by institutional check, even if the subscription is designated for an individual.) Standing orders are accepted.

Single copies are available at $6.95 when payment accompanies order, and *all single-copy orders under $25.00 must include payment*. (California, Washington, D.C., New Jersey, and New York residents please include appropriate sales tax.) For billed orders, cost per copy is $6.95 plus postage and handling. (Prices subject to change without notice.)

To ensure correct and prompt delivery, all orders must give either the *name of an individual* or an *official purchase order number*. Please submit your order as follows:

Subscriptions: specify series and subscription year.
Single Copies: specify sourcebook code and issue number (such as, IR8).

Mail orders for United States and Possessions, Latin America, Canada, Japan, Australia, and New Zealand to:
Jossey-Bass Inc., Publishers
433 California Street
San Francisco, California 94104

Mail orders for all other parts of the world to:
Jossey-Bass Limited
28 Banner Street
London EC1Y 8QE

New Directions for Institutional Research Series
Marvin W. Peterson, *Editor-in-Chief*

118,759

Contents

The Association for Institutional Research was created in 1966 to benefit, assist, and advance research leading to improved understanding, planning, and operation of institutions of higher education. Publication policy is set by its Publications Board.

PUBLICATIONS BOARD
Paul Jedamus (Chairperson), University of Colorado
Eugene C. Craven, University of Wisconsin System
William P. Fenstemacher, University of Massachusetts–Boston
Horace F. Griffitts, Tarrant County Junior College District
Marilyn McCoy, University of Colorado System
Normal P. Uhl, Mt. St. Vincent University

EX-OFFICIO MEMBERS OF THE PUBLICATIONS BOARD
Mary E. Corcoran, University of Minnesota
Charles F. Elton, University of Kentucky
Richard R. Perry, University of Toledo
Marvin W. Peterson, University of Michigan

EDITORIAL ADVISORY BOARD
All members of the Publications Board and:
Frederick E. Balderston, University of California, Berkeley
Howard R. Bowen, Claremont Graduate School
Roberta D. Brown, Arkansas College
Robert M. Clark, University of British Columbia
Lyman A. Glenny, University of California, Berkeley
David S. P. Hopkins, Stanford University
Roger G. Schroeder, University of Minnesota
Robert J. Silverman, Ohio State University
Martin A. Trow, University of California, Berkeley

Editor's Notes

Not long ago on a consulting visit, I was invited into an institutional researcher's storage room—four walls lined at least eight feet high with printouts. Always the idealist, I asked where the data went from there. There was a long pause: "Well, some data have been orally reported to executive administrators. These two we wrote up for committees. Others were summarized in our *I. R. Newsletter.*" That was about the size of it.

"What is on these printouts?," I asked. "Usual stuff—enrollment counts and projections, budget information, entering student profiles, couple attrition studies, student ratings of instruction. We did a nice little study of minority concerns, this stack over here, but seems to me we never had time to write it up. Shame. Some telling data in there."

Sound familiar? What good is institutional research to academic practice if it is not about meaningful educational questions and not moved from stored data into action? Certainly executives need "hard" data about financial well-being, and that aspect of institutional research is well-developed. But what plan is there for using institutional research to improve academic practices? Usually none. Institutional researchers hope to make a difference, but the subtleties of translating research into academic practices, the even greater subtleties of communicating such information to the faculty, and the practical pressures of "number crunching" for financial accountability (and, rarely, learning accountability) make the use of institutional research for improving academic practice a very difficult and marginal activity in most colleges.

The irony is heavy. Academic institutions value research. They value effectiveness in academic practice. Yet they do not value research to improve academic practices. Why? Abraham Maslow offers one answer—because effectiveness as a worry comes after survival, security, and acceptance. Executives (who own institutional researchers) must worry first about basic needs. Sad, in institutions ostensibly about especially truth as well as beauty and justice; but there it is. As the 1980s puts increasing survival pressure on postsecondary institutions, there it will be.

What can be done? It turns out, more than many institutional researchers have experienced. The chapters in this book discuss institutional research which does get used in academic evaluation and which does make a difference. The volume's purpose is to propose a conceptual framework and practical strategies for getting institutional research used to improve academic practices. It demonstrates how we can put systematic information behind four fundamental decision issues: (1) What do we hope to accomplish? (2) How are we doing? (3) What is keeping us from doing as well as we wish? and (4) How can we reduce those obstacles to greater success? Executive administrators, faculty leaders, and institutional researchers should find in this volume useful guidance for knowledge-based educational decisions.

The opening chapter by Lance Buhl and Jack Lindquist provides a conceptual framework for "action" research (jargon for research that gets used). Tom Hogan then describes, in Chapter Two, an action-research process his University of Wisconsin project uses to involve new academic program directors in developing evaluation data. Ernest Palola presents, in Chapter Three, a model and tips for institutional use of educational "Program Effectiveness and Related Costs" data. Aubrey Forrest, in Chapter Four, describes principles and practices for using learning-outcomes data. Stuart Terrass and Velma Pomrenke offer, in Chapter Five, "change agent" skills and strategies valuable in getting academic data used. I conclude in the final chapter with examples of quick, dirty, but useful action research.

Each chapter augments the view that systematic, involving strategies for research use can be done in postsecondary education and can help improve curriculum, teaching, and learning. This theory is familiar in practice, though research utilization is not in the lexicon of traditional institutional research. The cases in these chapters also should not seem bizarre to most institutional researchers. Bizarre is their happening, with any regularity, in colleges and universities. In this way, the authors offer fresh, rare insight into how institutional researchers can influence academic practices.

This is not the Bible. Some theory, some cases, some suggestions; but building the workable strategy is yours. The challenge for institutional researchers is formidable and basic to academic success in the 1980s. If we as institutional researchers do not present convincing evidence as to our educational effectiveness and do not get those data to improve educational practice, the Yahoos of simple-minded accountability will dominate higher education in the name of academic efficiency without meaning.

Jack Lindquist
Editor

*Jack Lindquist is president at Goddard College. Previously
he served as director of the Institute for Academic
Improvement at Memphis State University, the Kellogg Use
of Innovations Project at the University of Michigan, and the
Strategies for Change and Knowledge Utilization Project of
the Union for Experimenting Colleges and Universities. His
Ph.D. in higher education is from the University of
Michigan.*

*Action research offers an important framework and
guide for getting institutional research used, yet it
runs against the grain of the number-crunching and
written reports tradition of institutional research.*

Academic Improvement
Through Action Research

*Lance C. Buhl
Jack Lindquist*

Children pass through an orally inquisitive stage in which "Why,
Daddy?" and "Why, Mommy?" send parents into Socratic circles. Then
children grow up. They stop asking their parents why. They ask themselves, their peers, and the so-called experts: "Why do we need to change?"
"Why is this new idea of practice any better than the one we've got?" "If
this new thing is the answer to our prayers, what's keeping us from
implementing it?" and "When we do try it, how will we know if it works?"

These questions are not minor nuisances for educators or parents.
They point to essential issues. Unless academic leaders can help their
colleagues find impressive answers to such questions, improvement is
unlikely. Why go through the great bother and risk of change if there is no
apparent need, no convincing solution, and no evidence that the change
will succeed once attempted?

Enter *action research*. That phrase simply means what it says:
research designed to catalyze and inform action. It is research that helps us
answer those unavoidable "why's" with substantial "because's." Action
research is not intended, primarily, to advance scientific knowledge. It is
intended to provide individuals, groups, organizations, or communities

J. Lindquist (Ed.), *New Directions for Institutional Research: Increasing the
Utilization of Institutional Research*, no. 32. San Francisco: Jossey-Bass, December 1981.

with a sound knowledge base upon which to decide whether or not to change their ways. Action research is especially useful in helping faculty and administration clarify their sense of a need for change, identify resistances to change, and then plan to meet those needs and reduce those resistances. For colleges with unclear needs and likely resistances, action research can be a powerful resource for academic leaders. It is not a bad tactic for parents of inquisitive children, either.

Basic Tenets and Strategies of Action Research

Wendell French and Cecil Bell (1973) provide a general definition of action research as "the process of systematically collecting data about an ongoing system relative to some objective, goal, or need of that system; feeding those data back into the system; taking actions by altering selected variables within the system based both on the data and on hypotheses; and evaluating the results of actions by collecting more data" (p. 2). The social science jargon in that definition boils down to answering four common-sense questions: (1) What do we want to accomplish? (2) How are we doing? (3) What is keeping us from doing as well as we wish? (4) How can we reduce the obstacles to success? Action research not only helps generate information to answer these questions but also gets that information back to the questioners, helps them decide what needs to be done, helps them try out the new behaviors, and then aids their evaluation of the change. Action researchers, then, must play two roles: (1) they facilitate the gathering of systematic information concerning audience goals and problems as well as the means for resolving those problems and (2) they facilitate the information-based, problem-solving process itself. Action researchers are not just data-gatherers and analysts; they are also *facilitators*. It is this role, which is unusual for most researchers, that is crucial to making research useful.

The first tenet of action research is that individuals as well as organizations change by going through a rational problem-solving process like the one presented by John Dewey (1938). Dewey shows how we move from suggestions (formulating a problem or issue) to intellectualization (analyzing the problem) to hypothesizing (translating the problem into testable propositions) to reasoning (thinking through the consequence of the hypothesis) to, finally, experimentation (testing the hypothesis through action). Then we start all over by identifying problems that result from this action; thus, the problem-solving process usually is depicted as a continuous circle or spiral. This circle describes scientific method as well as the process by which we decide where to go for lunch.

Action research provides the systematic information and facilitation that make this problem-solving wheel go around. The second basic tenet of action research, then, is that problem solving is more likely to be successful if it is catalyzed, informed, and guided by experts in the gathering and use of information than if the process is "left alone." Individuals or organizations that do not readily solve their own problems are likely, claims action-research theory, to have inadequate information-gathering and -using skills and procedures. The institutional researcher who can facilitate knowledge use is a critical contributor to academic improvement.

A third tenet of action research is that no one else can solve our problems for us. If solutions are to fit our needs and situations and to represent our understanding and commitment, the problem-solving process must be "owned" by us, the researchers and research users. Action researchers therefore work *with* or *for* their clients rather than in ivory tower isolation from them. Action researchers do not tell their audience what the problem is and what the solution should be. They facilitate their audience as it decides these matters for itself. This tenet also leads to a conviction in keeping with the pragmatic tradition: the real test of truth is public. Clients validate action-research data by testing it against their own knowledge and judgment. Statistical tests for reliability and validity may be helpful to clients in drawing their own conclusions, but it is this public process of validation and decision making that lies at the heart of action research and the action researcher's responsibility. Later chapters confirm the importance of users' "owning" studies they are to use.

When the client is one person, as in an individual consultation in teaching improvement, the primary owner of the evidence, its validation, and the actions based on it is that one client. When the audience is a group or a whole organization, every member is regarded as a necessary owner. It is research and action "of the people, for the people, and by the people" who are concerned with or affected by change decisions. This democratic norm means that data are made available to everyone concerned rather than just to special elites, such as the executives. It means that collaboration between leaders and followers, executives and labor, administration and faculty, is the action-research way. It means that meeting the needs of each individual member is as important as meeting the needs of the organization as a whole. Indeed, the assumption is that the organization *is* its members. Without their understanding and commitment, effective improvement is unlikely. This is particularly true in such organizations as universities or hospitals where the essential "production" work is in the hands of professionals who usually do not like to be told what to do by formal authorities.

Many leaders are reluctant to be openly collaborative in problem solving because they believe that their clients or subordinates are closed, selfish people who, if given half a chance, will use available information and decision-making powers to enhance their vested interests at the expense of others. In this view, problem solving is a win/lose game: my gain is inevitably someone else's loss. Action researchers maintain that "my gain" can be *your* gain. If organization members take part in problem solving, they are likely to understand and support the resulting actions. This commitment is then likely to increase their contribution to the organizational mission, thereby creating a more satisfying and effective organization for everyone. Problem solving becomes a win/win process for all involved. Ensuing chapters in this volume will confirm that the competitive battle is less effective than collaboration in accomplishing measurable and enduring improvements or changes.

These tenets of action research lead to action-research strategies: First, data gathering has as its focus the client's problem-solving needs and processes. It generally attempts to garner evidence regarding the client's goals, problems in achieving those goals, and ability to resolve such problems. In particular, data gathering is concerned with *member perceptions* of goals and problems and with the *personal* or *interpersonal process* by which clients come to grips with, or avoid, those problems. Hogan's and Palola's chapters (Chapters Two and Three) dramatize the importance of building further inquiry from the concerns of one's audience.

Second, the whole research, feedback, and decision-making process is done with clients. They decide with the researcher what to study and why, how to study it, what the resulting data say, and what is to be done in consequence. The University of Wisconsin process described in Chapter Two is an exemplar.

Third, action research focuses the decision-making responsibility on the free choice of single clients or on the consensus of a group. This helps ensure the individual's commitment and understanding, which are vital to the success of any resultant changes.

Fourth, because regular and informed problem solving by clients is a major goal of action research (besides any particular actions that emerge from single interventions), facilitators regard themselves as educators and trainers who help the person or group become able to do action research on a continuous basis. Every contributor to this volume takes on that seemingly presumptuous but vitally important relationship to research users.

Action Research and Cultural Norms

These basic tenets and general strategies mark action research as quite different from most other kinds of research. These differences should become more apparent in later chapters as we suggest particular ways to carry out action research for academic improvement. But before we get into the details of this process, it might be wise to note the fit of action-research tenets with American cultural norms—with the rules and assumptions by which we act.

Certainly the democratic norm is an American ideal. Respect for individuals and the desire to involve them in decisions affecting them lie at the base of the democratic system. Moreover, our Christian tradition values giving, sharing, and helping rather than beating one's neighbor. We Americans combine both the pragmatic tradition, which tests truth against experience, and an intellectual tradition that values rational problem solving based on systematically gathered evidence. And our respect for rugged individualism places a value on solving one's own problems rather than on being dependent on some authority. It would appear that ours is an ideal culture in which to practice action research.

On the other hand, America is the home of the competitive spirit. "Winning is the only thing," Vince Lombardi said, and he was idolized for it. It is also the home of the hard-minded skeptic, the "show me" American who is not about to accept information that clashes with preconceptions unless the evidence is undeniable. We may believe in solving our problems together with genuine openness, but we also believe in solving our problems by denying and defeating the views of our opposition. Nowhere is this clash of norms as visible as in academic life. Academic people believe, on the one hand, in "shared governance" and "collegiality," in working things out together. They also believe in their own expertise and they work hard to convince others that their own view is the only correct one. Our intellectual tradition is that of the autonomous and isolated artist, poet, historian, chemist, or political scientist who works away privately until he or she enters a win/lose competition with colleagues. Committees that are supposed to work collaboratively are consumed in debates between unyielding, autonomous experts protecting their disciplinary turfs rather than moving toward the information and views of others.

McGregor (1961) calls this conflict of norms Theory X (people are closed, selfish, lazy, competitive) and Theory Y (people are, or can be if treated right, open, generous, motivated, and collaborative). Theorists and trainers such as Argyris and Schon (1974) as well as the Likerts (1967 and 1976) seek ways to help leaders behave consistently with Theory Y. The works of Lindquist (1978, 1980) and Sikes (1974) bring this tradition to postsecondary education. A major part of the action researcher's work is to resolve this conflict of assumptions about human nature in favor of Theory Y. Unless this work is successful, the tactics described on the following pages will break down. The research will stay unread or be used only to arm one group against another. For that reason, the use of a trained action-research consultant usually is necessary early in the process.

The Components of Action Research

There are several ways to conceptualize action research but we find Figure 1 a fair representation of a model helpful in introducing innovations. Action researchers gather and feed back information regarding each of the four information areas in that figure—needs, solutions, support, and

Figure 1

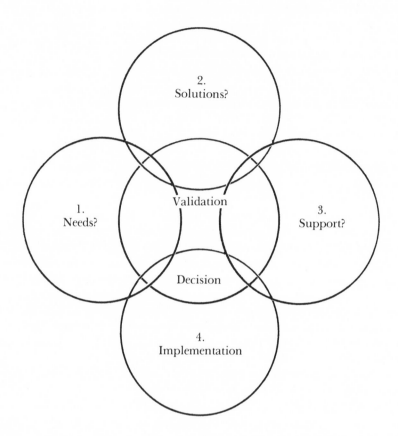

implementation. What are we trying to accomplish and how are we doing? How might we more effectively go about achieving our goals? What are the resistances to change and how might they be reduced? Once we decide to take up a new idea or practice, how can we learn whether it is working and what needs to happen to make it more effective? If helpful information can be gathered and used to answer these questions, improvements have solid grounding.

At the core of the action-research model is the process of validation and decision, the center of Figure 1. At each stage in Figure 1, information needs to be shared with the audience and the audience in turn needs to draw conclusions about the truth and make action decisions.

The developmental task facing the academic leader and researcher is to learn how to facilitate the data-gathering, feedback, validating, and decision-making process for each of the four information areas on Figure 1. The following practical guidelines and tips should aid that development.

Assessing the Need for Change. Few individuals or organizations change for the fun of it. They change because they feel a strong need to change, a "performance gap" between what they are now accomplishing and what they aspire to do. Several kinds of information can clarify that need. For each kind, alternative information-gathering approaches can be used. Figure 2 summarizes those information-gathering categories and approaches. Perhaps the most important point made by Figure 2 is that action-researchers would be wise to gather information about a variety of needs assessment categories by a variety of research means. No one category or method is likely to produce enough depth and breadth of perspective to yield a convincing picture of need among all the people who need convincing. This observation parallels the wisdom of conventional research methodologists. In operational terms, they refer to "triangulation of measurement," a very useful concept to bear in mind for action research: "Once a proposition has been confirmed by two or more independent measurement processes, the uncertainty of its interpretation is greatly reduced. The most persuasive evidence comes through a triangulation of measurement processes. If a proposition can survive the onslaught of a series of imperfect measures, with all their irrelevant error, confidence should be placed in it" (Webb and associates, 1966, p. 3). Harold Hodgkinson, discussing the evaluation of innovations in higher education, puts the idea in more positive terms: "different measures, coming from different sources, all indicating the same result, greatly increases the reliability of judgments based on the measurements" (Hodgkinson, 1981). In lawyers' terms, these various approaches can lead to a "preponderance of evidence" clearly pointing in one direction or another. We are thereby saved from generalizing on the basis of thin and slanted information.

Most action-research activities begin with data gathering to clarify desired outcomes and goals. What do you hope to accomplish? Why is that so important to you? Goals questionnaires and individual procedures such as in-depth interviews or life-planning exercises can help clarify goals. So can more indirect data such as (1) synthesizing various published statements of goals (at colleges, for instance, the admissions catalogue, course descriptions, and the president's annual report have goal statements), (2) recording how much time people spend in various activities (which suggests goal priorities), (3) noting which functions get the biggest budget or lushest carpets, and (4) observing which topics are most often discussed in formal and informal meetings.

Because people usually value more goals than there is time and money to pursue, a key action-research activity is to help establish goal priorities. Questionnaire or interview respondents may be asked to rank their top five goals or more specific objectives. Members of a goal-setting

Figure 2. Needs Assessment Categories and Kinds of Information

Categories

1. *Objectives and Outcomes*
   What are the results of this institution's or program's functions, and how do these match up to objectives?
2. *Clientele*
   What are the characteristics and needs of the people for whom this institution's or program's services (or products) are intended?
3. *Resources*
   What are the strengths and weaknesses of the staff, materials, facilities, and economic and political support available to produce those services or products?
4. *Functions*
   What are the strengths and weaknesses of the process by which resources are used to accomplish desired ends?

Kinds of Information

1. *Self-Reports*
   What needs are revealed by program staff and clientele themselves through such measures as journals and diaries, critical incidents, checklists, questionnaires, and interviews?
2. *Observations*
   What needs are revealed by outsiders who look at program clientele, resources, functions, and outcomes by such devices as direct observation of behavior, unobtrusive measures, audio and video taping?
3. *Records*
   What needs are revealed by a study of minutes, budget ledgers, and other program records?
4. *Products and Performances*
   What needs are revealed by analysis of papers, syllabi, job descriptions, tests, physical objects produced, and publications?

workshop may be asked to do the same. These priority assessments then can be ranked by quantity of time and other resources devoted to each goal. Particularly revealing can be exercises in which clients are forced to choose between two and three highly desirable goals. If you have one open position on a faculty and two candidates, each equally strong but in different areas (say, teaching and research), whom do you pick, all other things being equal? Or if you must choose between balancing the budget and going ahead with a desperately needed program by running a deficit and borrowing, what will you choose?

A "performance gap" arises when desires and realities do not coincide. Once action researchers have helped their audience to set goal priorities, the task is to generate evidence regarding current fulfillment of those missions. Do our graduates know what we want most? (This is the question Forrest uses in the action research he describes in Chapter Four.) Is our counseling service really used, and does it make a positive difference? Once again, self-reports from "users" of our services or products, observations of those people, records of events after "treatment" in our program, and performance tests of the persons or products produced by us offer a variety of perspectives by which to determine whether outcomes fit expectations. As Palola emphasizes in Chapter Three, when the same conclusion is produced from multiple perspectives, it becomes much more credible than when it is supported by only one point of view.

Assessment of the people served by an individual or institution is another important way to determine whether or not a need for change exists. Regarding college teaching, the question becomes, "What are the backgrounds and abilities, the interests and concerns, the learning styles and situations, of our students?" Often, program leaders know very little about their clientele, and action research may raise new needs simply by discovering that the program's objectives have very little to do with clientele needs or that the approach to serving those students has little relation to their style and situation. Classroom lectures in developmental psychology may look rather inappropriate for that mother of four who has great difficulty attending class (no available day care center or babysitting money) and who has worked in a mental health agency as an aid for fifteen years, or for the student who learns best not by lecture but through direct experience in the subject.

Once your audience has a rich picture of its goals, outcomes, and clientele, you need to provide a view of the resources that currently are used to produce services or products for that group. Again using the example of college teaching, we could ask such questions as what is the fit between the backgrounds, abilities, interests, styles, and situations of professors and those of their students? Do we have middle-class, white, independent, scholarly professors who have spent most of their time in schools and who are pressed to produce publications trying to teach poor, minority, inadequately prepared, dependent, career-inclined students who are "at home" on the job or the streets but not in school? Regarding facilities, do we have heavily mortgaged and inflexible classroom buildings and dormitories but a student body that must live at home, must work during most class hours, and is too poor or distant to afford commuting? Do we have rising costs in the face of declining income? Accreditation commissions formerly devoted most of their study to assessment of this resource category—the proper number and kind of professors, courses, requirements, standards, facilities, and equipment assumed necessary to produce quality education or research. It remains an important needs assessment category if combined with others.

A last focus of study that can be particularly revealing is what actually happens as the individuals or organizations function. Do professors mostly lecture and test for recall while students mostly take notes in class and memorize while studying despite the college's intention of developing active thinkers and creative inquirers? Do departments operate in great isolation from one another despite goals that stress production of an integrative whole? Is major staff-administrative conflict getting in the way of effective production? Many people draw conclusions regarding need for change by experience in the program in question. This "process" category of inquiry is especially helpful in showing these "experiential learners" whether their experiences and resulting concerns are representative of a larger group. Chapter Six shows specific ways to gather these kinds of descriptive data.

Assessing Potential Solutions. Too often, there is little evidence to suggest that one potential solution to a problem is any better than the status quo or other alternatives. Your administration and faculty may decide it has a problem that needs solving but that has no promising solution. Action research can help here. The task may be to ferret out fugitive data, such as buried evaluation reports or unreported institutional research, that can shed light on the relative effectiveness of one innovation over another. Or action researchers may turn to theory to suggest which approach appears more conceptually sound. If no data exists, action researchers may have to conduct their own study—for example, by interviewing and observing participants in three or four alternatives and by comparing available performance tests and products, as *Consumer Reports* does. Especially helpful is an experimentation center or pilot program in which alternative models can be tried and studied on a small scale before being considered for wider use. The academic leader who takes a few opinion leaders on a visit to innovative programs or who uses role playing and simulation to permit people to try out an innovation in a workshop setting is conducting action research, especially if that leader is systematic in facilitating careful data gathering, reflection, and action planning in those experiences.

In this study of alternatives, it is important to focus on key issues regarding how persuasive an innovation is to its audience. Does it promise to close our performance gap, to solve problems in pursuit of our objectives? How expensive in money and effort is it in comparison with the current approaches? Is it compatible with existing audience values, norms, structures, skills, styles, behaviors, authority? How simple is it to understand and do? Can it be adopted in part or modified, and how, in order to fit our situation? Many institutional researchers and academic leaders do not bother to put together solid evidence in answer to such questions, and even if they did, the answers would not be as credible as those generated by the audience itself with help from the researchers. New perspectives on innovation diffusion and knowledge utilization can be of great help to the action researcher (Lindquist, 1980).

Assessing the Climate Supporting Change. A real need and a promising solution are not enough to obtain change if the "system" is against it.

Blacks had real needs for equal opportunities and had seen promising solutions by the Nixon years, but then they fell strangely silent. If their needs had not been met, was it that they saw little hope that an attempt to change would gain the support under Nixon that it did under Kennedy and Johnson? Was there a diminished "sense of efficacy"?

Several factors are important in creating a positive environment for improvement:

1. *Leader Initiative and Skill* ("The Force"). Are there persons in high places who are actively pursuing such changes as the one in question, and are they skillful in raising need, interest, commitment, and resources for innovations?

2. *Linkage.* Are audience members well connected to the information, materials, and human skills they need to carry out problem solving?

3. *Openness and Tolerance.* Do many people actively seek to understand and appreciate new ideas, practices, or products? Are innovators respected and encouraged?

4. *Collaborative Ownership.* Do the persons responsible for, expert and participant in, and affected by current or new programs feel that these programs are solutions they value to problems they perceive in pursuit of goals they hold?

5. *Rewards.* Is the process of identifying needs, developing solutions, and carrying them out rewarding for those involved, both intrinsically and extrinsically?

These five factors, whose first letters spell FLOOR, are the building materials for the foundation of organization improvement (Lindquist, 1978). Questionnaires, interviews, observation, and analysis of records can be used to assess this part of the problem-solving equation. Also, a "force-field analysis," which asks audience members to list quickly on the left side of a blackboard or newsprint all the forces supporting a particular change and on the right side all the resistances to it, can build a picture of the climate faced by improvement leaders (Chickering and others, 1978).

Assessing the Implementation of Innovations. Assume for a moment that commitment to solving a problem and to a solution is sufficient in a climate hospitable to change so that a decision to adopt an innovation occurs. The action researcher's job is not near its end, for now comes the task of helping clients understand how implementation is going so that they can correct difficulties and judge effectiveness. The death or stunted growth of a change often occurs after its approval.

The major difference between this area of data gathering, feedback, decision making, and action and the other areas is specificity. Because a decision was made to make a particular change, to adopt a specific improvement, the evaluation of implementation can start by determining the objectives, resources, functions, and early outcomes of that innovation. Then, various research methods can be focused upon these needs, this solution, the climate affecting this solution, and these outcomes. Such evaluation might be rigorously "criterion-referenced"—that is, based solely on predetermined criteria for effectiveness. This approach lends clarity and intentionality to data gathering and decision making. But care should be taken to note criteria that emerge or change as implementors learn by doing. Rarely is there sufficient understanding before launching a new program to predict just what will or should happen. Unintended experiences and outcomes often are the most valuable and would be omitted from strict, objectives-based research. Thus, the action research described in the following chapters is, though focused, open-ended. In addition, Stufflebeam (1971) suggests that, when determining criteria for effectiveness, we should separate immediate outcomes such as participant satisfaction, successful program facilities or budgets, and the testing of participants or products just after program experience (the final exam syndrome) from longer-term outcomes such as the lasting value of participation or the enduring usefulness of products.

Evaluation is, as W. James Popham (1974 and 1975) reminds us, the "determination of value." Action researchers must be cautioned not to make that determination themselves. Program implementors, their review bodies, and potential dissemination audiences must make that judgment for themselves through the same validation and decision stages employed for other data-gathering and feedback stages. The action researcher's job is to get that determination to happen openly among all concerned.

One of the important issues to clarify in this process is whether or not these judges wish to use implementation assessments for *formative* purposes (to improve the new program) or for *summative* purposes (to decide its worth and fate). Daniel Stufflebeam (1971) argues that formative evaluation serves decision making to solve problems while summative evaluation serves decision making for accountability. Both are important, but the mind-set concerning each is different. It is one thing to ask, "How can we improve it?" and quite another to ask, "Is it worth keeping?" The first question is more in keeping with the problem-solving tenet of action research, but the second also needs to be asked and leads to another problem-solving question: "If it is not worth keeping, what needs to be done instead?" Action researchers can help implementors move to these improvement questions by returning to Point 1 on Figure 1, general needs assessment. Thus, the circle of data gathering and feedback continues.

It is standard procedure for formative evaluation to be done by program implementors primarily and for summative evaluation to be done by external judges and authorities. However, to be consistent with the action-research norms of collaboration, openness, and ownership, both kinds of evaluation should be shared by implementors and authorities together. Decisions must be made by all involved if the understanding and commitment needed to improve a program or to take on new problems is to exist. Action researchers will have to work especially hard to help those responsible for accountability judgments to validate evidence and make decisions *with* program participants, especially when those judgments regard hiring and firing, budget allocations, changes in policy, or the continuation of the program itself.

One of the hardest things to do in any area of action research, but especially in the evaluation of new programs, is to determine just what will indicate success. What concrete evidence will constitute a reliable and valid indicator that this thing is working or not and is worth the bother even if it does work? The problem is to find public evidence, to gather information that is a visible sign of effectiveness. For example, an implementation objective in a college teaching improvement program might be to help dependent learners toward independent learning. One set of indicators may be scores on pretests and posttests of intellectual and ethical development as the learner moves from dependence before the program toward independence afterward. Another indicator might be a teacher's report that she had to give highly specific assignments to George every week early in the program but that now George can contribute his own notions as teacher and student jointly work out assignments. Still another might be that a spot-check early in the program indicated that only 10 percent of the participants read anything related to the program but not formally assigned, while late in the program 40 percent were doing related but unassigned reading. Each of these indicators is concrete and shows a Time 1 to Time 2 shift. If judges (not action researchers, who *facilitate* judgments) agree that these are good indicators and settle on the issue of quantity (how many participants move how far), decision-makers should be able to reach common conclusions.

Of course, someone will ask whether an indicator shows the effectiveness of this innovation as compared to any other innovation. Rarely can control groups be established in field settings. Where they can, so much the better. Where they cannot, a good substitute is a detailed picture of program *process*. If a journal kept by our dependent student George or if an interview with his teacher records that, through his grappling with his reliance on the teacher, he becomes more self-directed, and if we can see in those moving pictures the slow taking hold of the learning process by George, evaluators can have greater confidence than otherwise that George's change was partially enabled by the program. In essence, action researchers need to "take judges to the movies" in order to share such concrete evidence of program process and effect.

Several tips can be helpful in encouraging implementors to become self-conscious regarding their own work so that they can spot implementation problems before they are overwhelmed and so that they can identify implementation successes before they get discouraged.

1. As much as possible, give the responsibility for monitoring the implementation process to the implementors. This can be a tremendous learning experience. Think about appointing project historians, even project anthropologists, who maintain the records and who occasionally do some "field" visiting with other members of the group or with people who are affected by the change. These visits should give the implementor a sense of other involved individuals' knowledge about, feelings toward, and perspectives on the project.

2. Use external evaluation consultants from time to time. The danger in overusing "experts" outside the innovation is that implementors may become overreliant on them and thus learn less than the optimum. Still, consultants who know their stuff, who (especially) are committed to the formative evaluation process, and who know how to work with groups about data can be very helpful.

3. Consider using instrumented evaluations. There are some good ones. For example, if one of the prime emphases of the project is on the group and organizational environment (interpersonal relations, communications, verbal patterns of interaction, and so on), Rensis Likert provides a marvelous device for periodic checking in *The Human Organization* (1967) and, with Jane Gibson Likert, in *New Ways of Managing Conflict* (1976). Something less than a "validated" instrument, but one as powerful as any, is that suggested by Martorana and Kuhns (1975). Its strength lies in periodic administration within the group about what the authors call *goal hiatus*—the discrepancy between where the project is, relative to achieving objectives, and where we thought it should be, and about the personal and extrapersonal forces that need to be enlisted to push the project forward. These instruments, by the way, focus on issues too often neglected in implementation evaluations: the climate within the program and the climate external to it. Without a supportive internal and external environment, especially at the interpersonal level, innovations will have great trouble succeeding. There are, of course, many other instruments, some useful and some not so useful. Choose whether to use instruments and which ones to use with great care as to the appropriateness of the information to be collected to the group's norms, values, and objectives.

4. Do not neglect anecdotal evidence. Do not be overwhelmed by the often dysfunctional need to have a lot of technically precise statistical information. Refer, if that occurs, to our later discussion of the distinction between statistical and phenomenological validation.

5. Hold periodic evaluation sessions with the implementors. This is worth underscoring here. Ownership and learning are at issue. Give the change project—the experiment—time to work. Expect incremental change, not sudden reversals in behavior. Expect setbacks. Use them for learning and correcting problem-solving opportunities. Learn to recognize

and appreciate the little achievements that are in the right direction. Delay that summative evaluation until implementors have had time to study their effectiveness and to make corrections, whether that implementor is a single staff member trying to improve himself or herself in order to receive a favorable performance review or a whole group hoping to achieve permanent status or broader use for their experimental program.

Data Feedback. Researchers traditionally design and conduct their studies by themselves, carry out analyses by themselves, write up their findings and recommendations by themselves, and present their conclusions by themselves. Their audience gets in on the act only at the tail end of the process. In consequence, the research must be sold after the fact to people who feel no ownership of it and who have not participated in the learning.

Action researchers work with their intended audience from the beginning. At three critical junctures, they collaborate with their audience in the research: (1) deciding the purpose and design of research; (2) making the preliminary analysis; and (3) conducting the final validation and making a decision about action. We will take up the third juncture later. Here, let us focus on the first two.

A first step in action research is to develop an agreement, perhaps even a formal "contract," between action researchers and clients regarding what should be studied, why, and how. What should be the purpose, focus, and design of the inquiry? What methods are appropriate? If audience leaders—for instance, key faculty, administration, and student leaders in a college—are involved from the start with data gathering so that it meets the concerns and learning styles within the institution, then action researchers are on sounder footing than if they have to guess in isolation about the appropriate data-gathering methods. Of course, the researchers bring their own expertise on what to study and how, so this agreement should be a collaborative one. Also in the agreement should be an understanding of the material resources and audience time committed to the process. Leaders will need to provide (1) respondent time; (2) design, administration, and analysis expenses; and (3) time for feedback, validation, and decision making. If clients are to join the action research, they must be willing to give time to interviews, to give permission for observation, to give time to feedback and action-planning workshops. Better to get firm commitments in the beginning than to try to scare up cooperation in midstream (although that later encouragement is likely to be needed too). Action researchers will need to persuade clients of the importance of this participative method, for it is not normal procedure and client leaders are very busy. But the involvement is worth the careful preparation it may take.

One interesting device is to ask leaders to experience action research themselves by filling out instruments that researchers score and return or by going through a data feedback simulation. They then can learn firsthand the worth of this approach and its results.

A second crucial tme to involve one's audience in the research is just after data have been collected and tabulated but prior to extensive expert analysis. In effect, the trick is to get the data and the audience together before a research expert comes between them. Instead of questioning the expert's credentials, methods, and conclusions, the audience goes straight to the unexpurgated evidence. The action researcher merely provides percentage responses, interview summaries and quotations, observation scores, and other quantitative counts or qualitative insights (including the researcher's own, but these should be clearly marked as "my impressions"). Presentation of data may be in short written reports targeted for particular audiences, but a workshop or extended meeting in which audience members can interact with the data and with the action researcher is preferable. A major agenda item at such meetings should be, "What further analyses and data collection are needed in order to get a good fix on our problem area?" Researchers can propose statistical analyses that, if approved, now have a bit of client understanding and interest to precede later feedback. Of course, some evidence may be so clear and redundant in this early feedback that actions are planned while further analysis proceeds. Action researchers need to guard against the conservative tendency to perpetuate study in order to avoid coming to grips with glaring problems.

Data Validation. The action-research model used in this chapter makes validation and decision making the centerpieces of the whole process. Typically, they are considered at one and the same time, almost as identical procedures. It is useful to separate the two because, on closer analysis, much of what theorists describe as decision making really has to do with the assigning of meaning to the data by members of the group. Decision making without deliberate validation may result in little action of consequence.

Validation is the determination of the meaning of data. The familiar interpretation of the process focuses on the properties of survey instruments and the data generated. Do the instruments yield data measuring what they purport to measure? The issue is an important one. Data validated through statistical analysis are likely to gain greater acceptance than untested data, provided the statistician is trusted and the statistics are made understandable to their audience.

But there is more to validation than the manipulation of numbers. There is a phenomenological side to validation as well as a technical aspect. Decision-makers must perceive that the data, independent of their statistical properties, are relevant to action planning. The data must lead to and inform options. The most extensive data can be pretty meaningless (for the purposes of action research) unless they lead to action.

Because there are excellent manuals about statistical validation but few about the process by which public validity is established, this section will concentrate on phenomenological validation. What is it? Gestalt therapists talk about the importance to the functional, productive system of the ingestion of "new material" (information of all sorts) by the individual. They urge clients to "chew on" the data deliberately, to break data down so that they can be digested and integrated into the system. The danger of swallowing new food whole is at least twofold: the person will either gag and reject it, or it will pass into or through the body in ways that will cause disorders of one sort or another. The analogy is apt. When data about the group are fed back to the group, each member needs to "chew on" the data deliberately—to test it for its appropriateness to the system and for its digestibility. A quick scan and filing of a research report won't do the job. Time for chewing must be built into feedback. This testing of the data is both rational and emotional. But only by careful mastication and digestion are new data absorbed functionally for the health of the system. In less colorful terms, data about the group must be "re-owned" by the group in order for action research to run its intended course. The task of the person managing action research is to walk the thin line between group rejection of the data and too hasty group acceptance ("introjection"). One buys trouble either way.

What are some useful ground rules for helping groups to "chew on" new information? The following list is not exhaustive, but it is sufficient. It breaks down into rules for the period prior to the feedback session where the whole group will validate (or refuse to validate) the data and rules for the session.

1. *Before the session:*
   A. *Know your instrumentation and your data.* It matters little whether you are using a validated and sophisticated survey feedback technique or a noninstrumented data-generating approach (a game, simulation, or laboratory encounter), you *should be an expert about the strengths and weaknesses of the instrument or approach and in arranging and discussing the data.* This expertise concerns what the data *can* say and how your audience best can determine what it *does* say.
   B. To help ensure that the client will take ownership, you should *avoid interpreting the data.* It is the client's job to decide what the data say. Your job is to facilitate that interpretation.
   C. *Consider the option of feeding the data back to members before the session.* A brief guide to interpreting the data, a summary of the evidence itself, and appendices including full data and technical details of the sample and the analyses can help prepare the most rushed and the most critically precise participant (but do not be so naive as to

assume that many will have read beyond the summary or introduction prior to the session).

D. *Get the data organized for feedback quickly.* Nothing gets in the way of learning like old, cold information.

E. *Plan the feedback session carefully.* Involve key leaders with you in deciding just what is to happen. A useful session design is to begin with a brief overview of the study's purposes, design, sample, and analyses to date, plus suggestions on how to analyze the data. Follow with in-depth validation discussions in small groups led by well-oriented and respected persons. Ask groups to draw a few major conclusions and write them on newsprint for other groups to see. Synthesize the reports into major topic areas and assign new groups to design action plans for pushing ahead on each topic. End with presentations of those plans and a general call to action. Anticipate the various possibilities that might occur when the group receives the data. Prepare for any eventuality and be open to adjustment even in the best-laid plans.

F. *Work to get all members* of the group committed *to attend* the feedback/validation meeting. Pay attention to schedules and pick the most convenient times. Persuade key individuals personally. Publish the date well in advance and do the RSVP and follow-up routines. If appropriate, have formal authorities do the inviting.

G. *Decide who else is immediately affected* by the nature of the data and the actions likely to be taken by the client (or clients) in response to new information (for example, students are affected by teaching data and staff by budget data). Work either to have them attend the meeting (by gaining the permission of the client *and* by thinking through the probable effects of their presence on group behavior) or to set up parallel validation processes with them.

H. *Establish a clear contract about objectives and agenda* for the session with the client. Do it well in advance of the session.

2. *During the session:* The major rule is to establish a conducive climate for group deliberation. *Be a facilitator.* Like all other motherhood statements, this one requires some specific behaviors to explain it.

A. *Test the contract worked out with the client in advance.* Make sure that people know what the session is about, what its objectives are, and how it should proceed. And, if the data were sent out prior to the session, test to see whether each person received them and has had a chance to work with them.

B. *Establish problem-solving ground rules.* Make them simple and highly visible. If the audience has some previous experience in the mode, have members suggest useful rules for the game.

C. *Briefly review the data and encourage clarifying questions.* A sound practice here (and in every group meeting where substance is at issue) is to keep all relevant data *public*. Permit all to see the data as well as the amendments, ranking, and winnowing of the data. Become a flip chart specialist or xeroxing expert—but be brief!

D. *Get clients to share reactions to the data.* It is particularly important here that you ask clients to look for strengths as well as weaknesses or, if you are concentrating on strategies, to look for advantages as well as disadvantages in the information. An important point here is to keep to the "motivating" discrepancies between what is and what should be. A slight discrepancy is too small and an extremely large one much too overwhelming to motivate group members to accept the validity of data and of the notion that change is warranted.

E. *Make interactions as close to one-to-one as possible.* It is easy to make critical public attacks on research, and these can stop a large group dead. Small-group or one-to-one interactions, in contrast, provide greater "air time" for participants and greater openness and flexibility in discussion. Experts can move from group to group to provide consultation as needed. This is the heart of the "chewing" process. Think about the advantages of various types of group configurations for sharing reactions: dyads, triads, fishbowl, panel, whole group. Whatever form you choose, remember the rules: (1) work to get each person involved in working with the information and in honestly responding to it from a personal perspective and (2) test validity (what in the data seems sound and what does not) with clients while they are present.

F. *Keep discussion focused on the data and the data's relevance for problem solving.* The thrust of this rule is not to avoid emotional reactions—they may be entirely relevant to interpreting the data— but to prevent "blaming," "scapegoating," or "denial" behavior and to prevent discussions from wandering away from the evidence or problem and into disjointed exchanges of opinion. The action researcher's highest group-facilitator skills will be needed here.

G. *Keep clients from jumping hastily into decision making.* The validating process needs its due and should not be rushed. It may take several hours for a group of six to gain the comfort, understanding, group effectiveness, and insight needed to use the data properly. Of course, ten groups of six may bring an audience of sixty to the same point in the same period of time while those sixty working in one group might not yet be beyond harangues.

Data-Based Decision Making. Action research, to repeat, is applied social science. Decision making is an integral aspect of the research design. In a general sense, to be sure, decision making occurs several times within each stage of the change cycle. We will deal here with the more formal steps by which validated information—need or problem statements, possible solutions, identified sources of support, alternative monitoring patterns—are translated into "go" or "no go" commitments to move on to the next stages of the cycle.

The consequences of failing to honor this formal decision-making process are not particularly functional for the group or organization. Think, for example, of "master plan" schemes. A new chief college administrator enters office and initiates a master plan. Often it is well conceived *through* the validation phase of at least Points 1 and 2 on Figure 1—that is, determining needs and solutions. Yet our usual experience is that nothing *happens* with the spiffy goals, objectives, forecasts, and "new dawning." Decision making by the validating "public"—other administrators, most of the faculty and representative students, maybe even some alumni and community members—is neglected (or more probably, unanticipated in the design to begin with). Inevitably, the result is frustration, a sense of disenfranchisement, a strong conviction that a lot of time and energy was wasted for very little return. Business as usual moves on. And certainly learning, especially as it relates to the validity of collaborative problem solving, is short-circuited if not fatally electrocuted. Let the same chief administrator try that ploy again with that group!

It is important to emphasize that putting decision making at the center of the action-research model reinforces the learning that precedes this step. The issues for decision making are, first, whether the validating client system wants to change and, second, if so, how it wants to go about changing. It is altogether possible, of course, that a client may decide not to change. Absolutely sufficient reasons may exist—the material and psychic costs seem too high, the gains not worth the effort, necessary resources unavailable, the evidence suggests no clear problem or solution. The point is that "no go" decisions and the reasons for them ought to be made deliberately by the client individual or group; the "no go" decision needs validation too. Similarly, the "go" decision ought to be arrived at just as deliberately. In this respect, decision making is the acid test of validation. How extensive and sincere is the commitment to validated information and to the choices already made? How many in the group are committed to action? How much behavioral support are they willing to give?

These questions underscore the fact that formal decision making involves more than a "yea" or "nay" vote about change. It is useful to think of the whole decision-making process as *action planning*. There are numerous versions of the action-planning sequence. Each is a hybrid, owing much of its form to one or more other versions. Accept the eclectic nature of action planning, which is another cyclical process, and you come up with something like the following:

1. *Define the specific goals and objectives to be accomplished.* In the terms of the action-research model used in this chapter, you are concerned here to get the group to select among validated information (needs, solu-

tions, sources of support, and evaluations) those ideas that seem most logically consistent as a package, most worthwhile, and most achievable.

2. *The next task is to translate the choices into goal and objectives statements.* For the record, a *goal* is a desired state. It identifies a purpose for actions. Though perhaps never fully realized, it serves as the pole star. An *objective* is a clear, concise statement of an outcome that, when achieved, will contribute to the attainment of one or more of the goals. To be most useful, a statement of objectives should take into account the *time frame* for action and the *criteria* (qualitative and/or quantitative) that will serve to let you and others know when the outcome has been achieved. Several objectives, logically sequenced, are often necessary to reach a goal.

Defining goals and objectives may be the hardest part of the planning process. Values are at stake. Take your time. Make sure that you attend to interpersonal process issues so that the resulting "product" of the client's work reflects the values and contributions of the individual or group. A powerful technique for working toward consensus is the *nominal group* process in which you get members of the group (perhaps in subgroupings of six to ten to *rank order* the data, discuss the results, rerank or weigh the data, and organize a final listing. Tom Hogan, in Chapter Two, describes this same ranking process used to decide what should be the topics of program evaluation.

A similar technique for reaching a consensus on goals is *Delphi forecasting.* The procedure in the Delphi format is an iterative process by which individual members of the group weigh or rank the data, compare and discuss their responses relative to the total group's response, reweigh and compare again, and at each point provide rationale for significant discrepancies betweeen their rankings and that of the entire group. Both the nominal group and the Delphi techniques have the advantages of using group problem-solving norms, organizing discussions around the data, and moving toward consensus. They are inappropriately used if individual members of the group feel they are being railroaded or coerced, if sufficient opportunity is not provided for discussion, or if the manager of the process does not understand the technique, does not know how to organize the data, or does not work within the limits of the technique.

3. *Organize strategies for action.* Because this action-research model suggests a sequence by which needs, solutions, sources of support, and monitoring devices should already be suggested by the group, this step may be self-evident. But it is important to emphasize that, as with the solution stage, alternatives ought to be considered *before* plunging into some action.

Develop an action flow chart for each strategy selected. The chart should have several characteristics: (1) it should be referenced to particular goals and objectives; (2) it should specify the tasks needed to reach each objective; (3) it should identify the persons who have been assigned and who have accepted responsibility for managing each task; (4) it should specify start-up, reporting, and stop target dates; and (5) it should define the criteria that will direct the strategy.

4. *Do some reality testing.* Testing for the reality of plans is the necessary counterpoint to the whole planning melody. Is there genuine consensus? Has enthusiasm, commitment, and willingness to take responsibility waxed or waned significantly? Is a disssenting group in the making? Has the client group determined whether it has the material resources, skills, energy, and support to accomplish objectives and goals? Has it taken care to identify probable obstacles both within itself and in the world "out there"?

An extremely useful approach to reality testing is *force field* analysis by which individuals or groups identify the forces—people, information, material resources, policies, norms, practices—that affect accomplishment of action plans. They decide which forces drive and which forces restrain the effort to achieve objectives. They then develop and test plans to make sure that assisting forces are taken advantage of and hindering forces are accounted for. Martorana and Kuhns (1975) have adapted Lewin convincingly to the higher education scene. Their discussion and illustration of group reality testing is particularly helpful.

Summary

If an academic group or individual is less than clear about a problem for which change is needed or if that audience has less than a receptive climate to support this change, action research is a useful aid to academic improvement. It helps audience members ("clients") to clarify their goals and needs, sort out the possible solutions, reduce obstacles to positive changes, and evaluate the effectiveness of these changes as they occur.

Action research differs from other research models in that it acts as an information catalyst and guide to practical problem solving. It also differs in stressing that both the research and the problem solving should be openly collaborative processes "owned" by the people affected and validated with their own experiences. This public validation and decision-making process is regarded as the core of action research. In consequence, the action researcher must be expert both in social science research and in facilitating the individual or group problem-solving process.

This chapter suggests four major foci for data gathering and feedback: assessing the needs, evaluating alternatives, assessing the support or resistance to change, and evaluating the implementation. At each of these stages, clients should be involved in developing and validating the information as well as in deciding what to do because of it. If such a process is developed, the prospect of informed, accepted, and effective institutional improvement should increase substantially.

References

Argyris, C., and Schön, D. *Theory in Practice: Increasing Professional Effectiveness.* San Francisco: Jossey-Bass, 1974.

Chickering, A., Halliburton, D., Bergquist, W., and Lindquist, J. *Developing the Curriculum: A Handbook for Faculty and Administration.* Washington, D.C.: Council for the Advancement of Small Colleges, 1978.

Dewey, J. *Experience and Education.* New York: Macmillan, 1938.

French, W., and Bell, C., Jr. *Organization Development: Behavorial Science Interventions for Organizational Improvement.* Englewood Cliffs, N.J.: Prentice-Hall, 1973.

Hodgkinson, H. Personal conversation with Lance Buhl, 1981.

Likert, R. *The Human Organization.* New York: McGraw-Hill, 1967.

Likert, R., and Likert, J. G. *New Ways of Managing Conflict.* New York: McGraw-Hill, 1976.

Lindquist, J. *Strategies for Change: Academic Innovation as Adaptive Development.* Washington, D.C.: Council for the Advancement of Small Colleges, 1978.

Lindquist, J. (Ed.) *Increasing the Impact.* Battle Creek, Mich.: W. K. Kellogg Foundation, 1980.

McGregor, Douglas. *The Human Enterprise.* New York: McGraw-Hill, 1961.

Martorana, S. V., and Kuhns, E. *Managing Academic Change.* San Francisco: Jossey-Bass, 1975.

Popham, W. J. *Evaluation in Education: Current Applications.* Berkeley, Calif.: McCutchan, 1974.

Popham, W. J. *Educational Evaluation.* Englewood Cliffs, N.J.: Prentice-Hall, 1975.

Sikes, W., Schlesinger, L., and Seashore, C. *Renewing Higher Education from Within.* San Francisco: Jossey-Bass, 1974.

Stufflebeam, D. *Educational Evaluation and Decision Making.* Istaca, Ill.: F. E. Peacock, 1971.

Webb, E. J., and Associates. *Unobtrusive Measures: Nonreactive Research in the Social Sciences.* Chicago: Rand McNally, 1966.

Lance C. Buhl is president of Projects for Educational Development, former executive director of the Professional and Organization Development Network, and an independent consultant. His Ph.D. in history is from Harvard University.

Jack Lindquist is president at Goddard College. Previously he served as director of the Institute for Academic Improvement at Memphis State University, the Kellogg Use of Innovations Project at the University of Michigan, and the Strategies for Change and Knowledge Utilization Project of the Union for Experimenting Colleges and Universities. His Ph.D. in higher education is from the University of Michigan.

118,759

LIBRARY
College of St. Francis
JOLIET, ILL.

How does action research really work? Here is a
practical example from a statewide project to evaluate
a set of nontraditional programs in higher education,
with some tentative conclusions about the strengths
and weaknesses of the action-research approach.

The Wisconsin
Evaluation Project

Thomas P. Hogan

Buhl and Lindquist, in their introductory chapter to this volume, com-
mend to the reader an approach to institutional research or program
evaluation that they label "action research." In addition to providing a
rationale for this approach, they offer a series of practical suggestions as to
how one might go about implementing an action-research program. This
chapter is a natural extension of their effort: it describes one particular
program evaluation that was designed from the beginning to incorporate
many of the characteristics of action research. The program evaluation to
be described here was not, however, intended to be a "test case" for action
research, nor was it articulated with any particular description of an
action-research model. It simply grew up, spontaneously one might say, in
response to the same set of concerns that has led to the formulation of the
action-research model. It might be helpful, then, at the outset to outline
briefly what these concerns were.

The Crisis in Educational Research

There seems to have developed within the past several years a general consensus that educational research is in a state of crisis. Despite the
great refinements in methodology and measurement, the infusions of

J. Lindquist (Ed.), *New Directions for Institutional Research: Increasing the*
Utilization of Institutional Research, no. 32. San Francisco: Jossey-Bass, December 1981.

"accountability" dollars, and a public sentiment largely in favor of hard-nosed evaluation of educational programs, the simple fact of the matter is, as nearly everyone has concluded, that educational research does not make a difference (see Braskamp and Brown, 1980; Alkin, Daillak, and White, 1979). More specifically, decision-makers do not use evaluation results as a basis for making decisions. Educational research, it appears, has in most instances become a game people play, which is taken seriously on the face of it but is unrelated to the real day-to-day concerns of the participants.

This is a strange turn of events, indeed. Early in this century, when the foundations of educational research were being laid by E. L. Thorndike, James McKeen Cattell, and their colleagues, the promise of educational research was great. Education, an ancient art, would be brought into the scientific age. Educational decision-makers, including teachers, administrators, legislators, even students themselves, would soon be able to make their educational decisions on a sound, scientific basis. Educational literature of the age was full of this hope. The world at large bought the promise. Then, with the huge increases in expenditures for educational research in the 1960s, it seemed that the promise would finally be fulfilled. It wasn't. Nothing really happened. Evaluation experts were crestfallen, legislators were angry, educators harumphed, and the world went on as usual. Decisions were still made largely on the basis of fads, fiscal pressures, personal interests, and hunches.

What went wrong? And how could one go about correcting the situation? Of course, to ask these questions, at least as they are worded here, belies a number of critical assumptions about the educational world, assumptions that we had best lay out on the table before proceeding. First, it is assumed that educational research *ought* to make a difference, that it ought to be a very important determiner of educational decisions, if not the sole determiner. Second, there is the assumption here that we *can* make educational research work—that educational research *can* influence decisions. Furthermore, it is assumed that those people who design and conduct educational research are capable of effecting the changes that will lead to utilization of this research. In other words, "effecting utilization" is not a matter of chance nor of powers beyond the researchers' control. Finally, in all the discussions of "what went wrong" there appears to be a tacit assumption that the basic model for educational research, and particularly for program evaluation, is essentially correct.

While all of these assumptions are fundamental, only the last assumption has received critical attention by the educational research community. It will be helpful, therefore, to sketch what this basic model for program evaluation is, as it is expounded throughout the land in textbooks and lectures on "how to evaluate educational programs."

The Classical Evaluation Model

The classical evaluation model proceeds through the following six steps: (1) identify and operationalize the program objectives, (2) identify appropriate measurement techniques or indicators, (3) specify how data is to be collected (the *research design*), (4) collect the data, (5) analyze the data, and (6) prepare a final report, summarizing all of the previous steps and emphasizing whether or not the objectives have been met.

In the most typical implementation of this model, the "evaluator" is solely responsible for completing each step. The evaluator will usually depend heavily on formal written documents from the program to identify objectives, although one or two meetings with project personnel will often occur at this stage. The evaluator then completes Steps 2 and 3 in relative isolation from project personnel: after all, the evaluator is the expert in these arcane matters.

Data collection and analysis (Steps 4 and 5) will be carried out either directly by the evaluator or under his or her supervision.

And then comes the piece de resistance: the final report, a quasi-dissertation type document, replete with null hypotheses, F-tests, hopefully some multivariate analyses, and (drum roll) *the* conclusion as to whether or not the project objective was achieved. One copy of the report goes to the project director and one copy is held by the evaluator, who immediately starts considering what kind of publication possibilities the research might have. This report is typically submitted two to four months after some benchmark date for the program (such as the end of the first or second year) and about six months after some decision-makers have decided to continue the program, modify it, or scrap it altogether.

This is the model that doesn't work—not that it can't or shouldn't work, but in plain fact, it doesn't work.

Recent work in the field of educational research has concentrated on two types of remedies for this unfortunate state of affairs. First, a number of writers have been questioning whether the basic model outlined above is the only appropriate one for all types of program evaluation. Stake (1976) and House (1978) have presented summaries of alternative models for conducting program evaluations, with an emphasis on the viewpoint that the model selected for use may vary depending on the purpose of the evaluation (*purpose* is defined here in terms of the types of decisions to be made) and the audiences for the evaluation results. Popham and Carlson (1977) and Thurston (1978) focus on one of these alternative models, the so-called adversary model. But, although the alternative evaluation models summarized by these authors are thought-provoking, they are rarely used. Only the "classical" model outlined above and the self-study or "blue-ribbon panel" model—which are perhaps more outgrowths of a rhetorical tradition than of a scientific tradition—have been used with any frequency.

The second major attack on the problem of nonutilization of evaluation results has centered on the final step in the classical model presented above, the reporting step. It is this step that Harold Howe (1976) seems to have had in mind when he claimed that educational researchers "won't succeed in the mission of causing useful change unless they learn to communicate with the people who must carry it out."

Howe, of course, was not alone in recognizing that communication was perhaps *the* problem in nonutilization of evaluation findings: the entire educational research field has witnessed a veritable stampede of diffusion and dissemination efforts, and unemployed English majors all of a sudden have found openings in educational R and D centers. This has, by and large, been a very happy development: it's nice to read an educational research report that is both accurate and understandable. It is not that highly technical reports are unnecessary; they are very necessary for certain purposes and audiences. Now, however, educational research has recognized that there are purposes and audiences besides those for which the technical reports are designed. (Palola, in Chapter Three, provides some practical suggestions regarding the design of reports for varied purposes and audiences.)

Despite the fortunate developments we are witnessing in the reporting area, it must be admitted that these developments relate to only one step in the classical evaluation model—the last step. While the evaluator may permit, even encourage, variegated reporting of a program evaluation effort, the evaluator is still firmly in control throughout the first five steps of the process. Having noted some felicitous consequences of diversification at Step 6 (reporting), we might reasonably ask: What would result from similar efforts aimed at Step 1 through 5? Suppose the evaluator is not in total control throughout these steps. With whom might responsibility for completing these steps be appropriately shared? And what are the practical implications of attempting to share such responsibility? These are the types of questions I wish to address in this chapter, but, before I do so, let me describe the context of the project in which these questions were treated.

The Wisconsin Context

The 1970s witnessed the rapid development of numerous nontraditional degree programs aimed at adult students. These programs offered great flexibility in study opportunities with respect to time and place, and they often featured characteristics such as credit for prior learning, individually designed majors, and competency-based curricula. In 1976, the University of Wisconsin (UW) system, consisting of some 150,000 students scattered among thirteen four-year campuses and fourteen two-year campuses, committed itself to the development of extended degree programs.

These programs were aimed at adult learners who, because of family or job responsibilities or geographic location, could not complete an on-campus degree program. The extended degrees were to be competency based, allow for crediting prior learning, provide for use of diverse learning modes, feature the use of contracts, and begin on a firm financial basis.

Perhaps most importantly for our purposes in this chapter, each extended degree program was to be developed and administered by one of the individual campuses within the system. There would not be one central office controlling all of the extended degrees, any more than there was one central office controlling all of the English departments or business schools in the UW system. Hence, decision making regarding the programs' operation would be decentralized.

By 1978, three extended degree programs became operational (general studies at Green Bay, business administration at Platteville, and an individually designed major at Superior) and several other programs were in advanced planning stages (agriculture at River Falls, vocational education at Stout, associate degree program within the two-year Center System, and home economics at Madison). As the program moved toward operation, questions were raised with increasing frequency about how these new programs would be evaluated, what kind of quality control would exist, and what kind of information would be needed in order to modify the programs. Interestingly, exactly the same questions (but expressed in different tones of voice) were being raised by such varied groups as advocates of the programs, skeptics, and neutral bystanders.

As these questions were asked, discussions began among the extended degree program personnel and the staff members of the Wisconsin Assessment Center at UW/Green Bay about a plan for attacking the questions. The plan was formalized under the code name EDCAP (Extended Degree Comprehensive Assessment Plan), but it is referred to in this chapter simply as the Wisconsin evaluation project, and it was eventually funded for two years of developmental work by the U.S. Office of Education. It is this project that is described in the following sections as an example of an action-research approach to program evaluation.

The Participants

The action-research model for evaluation might also be labeled the *participant* model since program personnel play such a key role in planning and executing the evaluation. Of course, there are participants in the classical evaluation model, too: program personnel who are thought of as clients, passive participants who are to be served, and evaluation experts (consultants) who plan and execute the evaluation. These roles change critically in an action-research approach.

In the Wisconsin evaluation project, three groups of participants may be identified. First, there were extended degree program personnel. Each campus offering an extended degree, or having one in an advanced developmental stage, was asked to designate one person as campus representative for the project. These campus representatives constituted the key decision-making group for the evaluation effort. Final decisions regarding what was to be evaluated, approximately how and when it would be evaluated, and other such "policy" issues rested with this group, thus making it analogous to a board of education or corporate board of directors. Interestingly, in nearly all instances, the extended degree program director chose to fill the role of campus representative rather than to delegate this responsibility to someone else, a fact that testifies to the importance assigned to this group.

A second group involved in the Wisconsin project consisted of several individuals from the Wisconsin Assessment Center who had originated the project but who were not directly affiliated with any one extended degree program. Although these individuals were evaluation experts, serving frequently as evaluation consultants for a wide variety of educational programs, their role in the Wisconsin project could most accurately be described as that of *managers* rather than consultants. As project managers, they implemented the general plans laid by program personnel (campus representatives), saw that appropriate issues were brought before program personnel, and generally kept the project moving along.

A third group in the Wisconsin evaluation project was an advisory panel, consisting of four individuals from outside the University of Wisconsin system who had considerable experience in nontraditional higher education, particularly from an evaluation perspective. By no small coincidence, three of the advisory panel members are contributors to this volume: Jack Lindquist, Ernest Palola, and Aubrey Forrest. The fourth member was Sister Georgine Loacker, codirector of assessment at Alverno College and a former member of the Council for the Advancement of Experiential Learning (CAEL) Board of Directors.

The advisory panel served two official functions. First, the panel members provided guidance by making available their experience and perspectives on evaluation of nontraditional education, by pointing out useful sources of information, by suggesting possible evaluation strategies, and by helping the project to avoid unnecessary parochialism. Second, the panel served an evaluative function: it evaluated the project itself, thus fulfilling a requirement incurred by the external funding of the project and more importantly, extending the guidance function beyond that of merely making suggestions to making judgments about the project's progress.

Virtually any evaluation effort will involve the first two types of groups identified above: personnel from the programs being evaluated and individuals external to those programs, ordinarily with some evaluation expertise, who will carry out the evaluation. The critical difference between the consultant approach to evaluation and the action-research model is in the roles played by these two groups. In the multicampus Wisconsin project, program personnel naturally originated with the participating campuses: there were really a half dozen programs being evaluated simultaneously. It is conceivable that this same general approach would function with just one program or with a much larger number of programs, although for practical reasons one would wonder about the feasibility of the operation with more than, say, twenty programs.

The availability of a highly respected, geographically dispersed advisory panel was a benefit made affordable by the external funding of the Wisconsin project. Obviously, in other circumstances, one might have to forego this benefit, although it may be possible by limiting geographic dispersion and frequency of advisory meetings to sustain many of the advantages derived from an external advisory panel without incurring substantial costs.

In addition to the three types of groups involved in the Wisconsin project, one might consider the inclusion of a fourth group—the administrators who, while not directly involved in the operation of the programs being evaluated, have some higher-level responsibility for supervision of the programs. It is often these types of individuals who will decide the fate of the program: its continuation or demise, its expansion, contraction, or reorientation. And such individuals may have a somewhat different set of evaluation needs than those of program personnel involved in the daily operation of the program. We have not systematically explored the role that might be played by such a fourth group.

Getting Started

An action-research program does not spring spontaneously into operation. At least you can't count on that happening, especially since decision-making power is deliberately diffused and those vested with decision-making power, namely the program personnel, are often bewildered by the field of evaluation with its occult aura of statistics, research designs, computers, and assorted other imponderables. So what steps can be taken to get the ball rolling? There are, we suggest, four things that must be done: (1) complete a background study in the area, (2) establish goals (what will be evaluated), (3) set priorities (which goals deserve the most attention and when), and (4) agree on ground rules for operating. Those happen to be the same four things that must be done under the consultant model, but they will be done differently under the action-research model.

In the Wisconsin project, we began with the preparation of a background paper—a hundred pages or so—on the evaluation of nontraditional higher education. The paper outlined possible strategies, identified existing instruments, mentioned similar projects, and discussed special problems. Ordinarily, evaluation consultants would complete such a study (or have it in their heads) and then proceed to draw up an evaluation plan. In the Wisconsin project, in contrast, this paper was simply distributed to program personnel for their consideration. The paper did not even conclude with a suggested plan of attack; that was to be drawn up by the three participant groups.

The grand scheme for the evaluation effort was developed at a two-day meeting attended by the three participating groups. The first part of this meeting allowed for a freewheeling, undirected discussion of what program personnel saw as important features of the evaluation—both what should be evaluated and how it should be evaluated, without, at this point, attempting to resolve all the details. While the focus of attention during these discussions was on the felt needs of program personnel, the advisory panel members contributed immeasurably with suggestions, observations, and clarifications.

A project manager's skill in guiding small-group discussion can be strained to the limit at this stage. The manager must be primarily a listener, not predetermining the outcome of the discussion (this initial meeting is not a "con" job to implement the consultant model surreptitiously) but still directing the discussion so that everyone speaks his or her piece without having any one person be overbearing.

At some point, it should become reasonably apparent that all the issues (the needs of program personnel) are out on the table, albeit in a discombobulated mass at the moment. Time for a break, during which the project manager assembles all of the various notions covered in the discussion into some type of orderly list of evaluation goals or topics. Each goal might be represented by a cryptic title and a brief (two or three sentences) description. When participants reconvene, this list is presented as a summary of the preceding discussion; a brief time is taken to see if anyone feels that something has been omitted or distorted. Note that at this point no one is claiming that all of these topics must be covered nor that everyone agrees as to their importance.

The group is now ready to establish some priorities. In the Wisconsin project this was accomplished by having participants, working separately, assign point values to each of the possible evaluation topics, first, in terms of the long-range, overall, "theoretical" importance of the topic, and, second, in terms of what information needed to be obtained immediately. Our list included twelve topics and the two-part rating of their priority was completed in short order. These ratings were quickly summarized by project staff and, presto, we had (1) a list of all major evaluation concerns, (2) an indication of the relative long-range importance of each concern, and (3) a priority listing of what should be attacked first and what could be delayed until later.

It is not the intent of this chapter to provide a description of the substantive content of the Wisconsin project but to describe the methodology used. Hence, we will not dwell on the actual results of the priority-setting session; a description of those results is provided by Kaiser, Mishler, and Hogan (1981). Figure 1, however, does provide a very condensed summary of the topics identified for evaluation and the ratings assigned to their long-range and immediate importance.

The fourth step in this "getting-started" stage of the project was to establish ground rules for operating. This step was completed through discussion regarding the respective roles of the three groups, a review of budgetary constraints, and similar issues.

Providing program personnel with background information about evaluation efforts related to their program, either in written form (as done in the Wisconsin project), by way of a seminar, or through some other means, is probably essential for generating discussion about the program personnel's evaluation need. Taking the "tabula rasa" approach, thinking that you will get a purer indication of program personnel's felt needs if their minds are not prejudiced by previous work in the field, would probably inhibit rather than foster open discussion. Examining other people's ideas is more likely to clarify and stimulate than to obfuscate and dull one's own thinking.

The initial priority setting does not need to be accomplished in one meeting. We attempted to complete the priority setting in one meeting because of the geographical dispersion of the group and the need to meet an externally dictated schedule. If one or both of these constraints is removed, it might be preferable to extend the priority setting over two or three meetings. Frankly, we were probably lucky to accomplish what we did in one meeting. Also, it might be possible to complete several of the later steps in the process by mail, although having personal interaction throughout the entire process is quite valuable.

Meetings—Their Frequency and Nature

Establishing the nature and frequency of meetings may seem horribly nitty-gritty. When describing a research procedure, one hardly needs a section on "when to think about it" because, quite simply, the researcher thinks about it whenever he or she finds it convenient. But the participant model being described here, as should be clear by now, does not operate at the researcher's convenience. If the participants are to engage in considerations of issues, make decisions, and lay plans, they must be brought together in some fashion.

In the Wisconsin project, these meetings occurred about every four months during the first year of operation, then moved to a semiannual schedule thereafter. In retrospect, that pattern seems to have been satis-

Figure 1. Items in Need of Evaluative Attention—The Wisconsin Project

	Ratings	
	Long-Range Importance	*Immediate Importance*
Student Outcomes: Program Learning (Are students learning what they are expected to learn?)	9.5	6.8
Student Outcomes: Graduate Follow-up (What happens to the students after graduation?)	9.3	4.1
Cost Studies (What are the costs of operating the nontraditional program?)	8.6	5.2
Student Flow, Progress (How do students progress through the program? And what are their difficulties?)	8.2	7.4
Acceptance, Image (What is the image of the program to faculty, staff, employers, others?)	7.9	5.6
Student Characteristics (Get an accurate description of the students in the program.)	7.1	9.1
Assessment of Prior Learning (Is the procedure for assessing prior learning a high-quality program?)	7.0	7.6
Learning Modes (What methods of learning are employed and with what success?)	7.0	7.0
Faculty, Staff (Get an accurate description of how faculty and staff function in the program and how the program affects them.)	6.9	6.1
Enrollment, Markets (Find new markets for the program and check on effectiveness of marketing strategies.)	6.8	7.9
Institutional Impact (What impact has the nontraditional program had on other parts of its host institution?)	6.4	4.4
Entrance Procedures (How effective are the procedures for introducing new students to the program?)	5.0	8.6

Note: Ratings were made on a 10-point scale, where 10 was high and 1 low.

factory, although it might be noted that the original projection called for continuing the pattern of meeting approximately every four months; as we moved into the second year, however, there was a general feeling that the semiannual pattern was adequate.

Each meeting lasted for one and one-half days and, with the exception of the very first meeting (described above), each was guided by a well-structured agenda prepared by the project manager. Agenda items fell into three categories: review, planning, and reporting. The review item is easily described: each meeting commenced with an update by the project manager on the overall progress being made in the project.

Planning items dealt with developmental work on one particular evaluation topic, from its original conceptualization, through drafting instruments or protocols, to designing data collection schemes. Of course, not all of these steps were completed for any one topic in a single meeting; sometimes the planning process spread over three or four meetings. But the entire planning process was brought before and discussed by the entire set of participants.

Reporting sessions were quite straightforward. After an evaluation study was completed, it was presented—by the project manager or a program director—to the entire group for discussion. Of course, much of the work accomplished at these meetings was buttressed by activities occurring between meetings: these activities will be described in the next section.

Bringing participants together physically for purposes of planning, reporting, and reviewing seems to us essential for the success of an action-research evaluation. Meeting vicariously, by way of mail or bits of electronic wizardry, may work with some groups and in certain types of circumstances. But these means of communication are perhaps too cold to allow the action-research model to flourish readily. Our meeting schedule (every four to six months) was dictated by a myriad of details quite specific to the Wisconsin project. One could easily imagine the use of alternative schedules in other circumstances.

Between Meetings

While meetings of participants are the building blocks in an action-research evaluation, what goes on between meetings is the cement that holds the blocks together. Since the meetings are primarily oriented toward discussion, if we had only meetings not much evaluation work would get done.

Actually, with a few exceptions, what goes on between meetings is not very different in the participant model than in the consultant model of evaluation. Instruments are refined; specific plans for data collection are laid; computers whir; drafts of reports are prepared; budgets are filed;

proposals for attacking new areas are circulated; and so on. All of these tasks involve the project staff and the managers. In the action-research model, however, program personnel are more frequently involved in actual data collection and in the preparation of written reports than in the consultant model.

In Wisconsin, much of the between-meeting work was carried out by members of the Wisconsin Assessment Center staff; however, at any given time each campus or program had one or more individuals working on some aspect of data collection. In some instances there was frequent contact among these individuals and project staff, while in other instances the individuals worked very much on their own. All results of this between-meeting work, of course, came back to the full group of participants at the next general meeting. Preparation of reports was also a shared responsibility. In some instances reports were prepared by project staff, in other instances by program personnel, and in still other instances there was joint authorship.

While there are individuals who derive a kind of masochistic delight in sheer data collection and in writing evaluation-oriented reports, these tasks are generally conceded by humankind to be drudgery. Hence, the extent to which participants share in these tasks is probably a good measure of the success one has had in implementing an action-research program. Involving participants only in planning the evaluation probably will not produce all the benefits of an action-research program. Going the next step and involving them in data collection, interpretation of results, and report writing is highly desirable, if not essential.

"Concluding" the Evaluation

The crowning glory of an evaluation effort in the consultant model is the "final report." In contrast, the crowning glory in the action-research model, in a way, is *not to have* a final report. Rather, the evaluation effort is seen as an ongoing process. It is not that questions are never answered but that questions are *continually* answered. There is a continuing flow of evaluative information, answering recurring questions, seeking original answers to newly formulated questions, and responding to the changing complexion of the program as it goes from year to year. For a program director, it might be said, there is no end to the need for evaluative information, although this is not meant to suggest that program personnel are to be buried in a blizzard of reports.

The Wisconsin project was conceived as a two and one-half year endeavor for purposes of federal funding; that is, funding was provided for the initial developmental work. However, for purposes of implementation, the project was not viewed as having some termination date. It will, simply, go on as long as the extended degree programs go on, although we are not so naive as to think that the project might not change drastically in character as a result of some presently unforeseen circumstance. While the project does not aspire to a "final" report, the reports do, in fact, keep flowing. At the present time, two or three formal reports are distributed in connection with each general meeting. We anticipate that this rate of flow will continue for a number of years.

It is conceivable that an action-research approach would result in the issuance of a "final" report. This would depend on the nature of the program being studied and the purpose of the evaluation. However, the action-research approach seems particularly suited to producing a continuous flow of information over a relatively long period of time.

Cooperation And Independence

Some evaluation projects deal with only one program and one group of program personnel, while other evaluation projects encompass several related or similar programs with a number of groups of program personnel. In the classical model of evaluation, there is a strong tendency, when dealing with a number of related programs, to extract what is common to all the programs, build a single evaluation scheme, and treat the various programs as replications of one program, or, failing that, treat the programs as entirely distinct, with each calling for its own evaluation scheme.

In the Wisconsin project, employing the participant model, we have forged a rather curious and dynamic balance between cooperation and independence. Without attempting to force either total cooperation or total independence, here is what, in fact, seems to have emerged. Through the priority-setting stage, program personnel seemed content with a predominance of cooperation. There appeared to be some security in a *group* identification of what was important. And, two years after the priority-setting exercise, this contentment with the group-established priorities seems to endure. Furthermore, through the first several cycles of evaluation work, cooperation (that is, everybody doing the same thing at the same time) seemed to predominate. This probably occurred because the topics with highest immediate priorities were high on everyone's list.

However, as time wore on, we noticed a move toward more independence. While everyone was still working within the same set of priority topics, some people wanted to move ahead with one topic while other people preferred another topic. This development seems to have occurred for two reasons. First, as we move down the priority listing of topics from highest priority items to intermediate priority items, there is a greater diversity of opinion. This is almost a statistical necessity: in order for an item to be very high (or very low, for that matter), it must be very high (or low) in nearly everyone's ranking, whereas an intermediate priority may result from a mixture of high and low ratings. Second, since much of the evaluative work was cumulative, it soon became apparent that with everyone doing everything we were becoming overburdened with evaluation activities.

Thus, as we moved into the second year of evaluation work, the various programs began to act more independently. For example, one program might be working on topics 3, 5, and 8, while another program was working on 5 and 9. This allowed us to cover a great deal more territory than with the "total cooperation" approach while we still kept the effort within reasonable bounds. The results of independent activity were always reported back to the full group so that everyone learned from each bit of evaluation. And, of course, some parts of the evaluation were still carried out by all programs at once.

We hesitate to predict that every application of the action-research model will move from the fully cooperative mode to a mixed cooperation/ independence mode. There is probably no reason to prefer one type of emphasis over another; yet, on the other hand, some minimal degree of cooperation is needed in order for the project to have any cohesiveness, while, on the other hand, some degree of independence fosters participant commitment to the project. In addition, fostering at least a minimal degree of independent activity seems desirable at this particular point in the history of higher education in order to help combat what Dressel (1980) labels the "erosion of autonomy" in public colleges.

Tentative Conclusions About Action Research

It is, of course, risky to draw general conclusions about the validity or utility of some approach based on one experience with it. However, it is also foolish *not* to attempt some analysis of the lessons to be learned from experience—even one experience. With that conflicting set of guidelines in mind, we attempt here to draw some very tentative conclusions about the strengths and weaknesses of the action-research approach, at least as it has been implemented in the Wisconsin project.

The special characteristics of the action-research approach are perhaps best described not in an absolute sense but in contrast to some other approach—specifically, to the "outside evaluation consultant" approach in which an individual or group conducts an evaluation of the program largely, and deliberately, without the influence of the people who operate the program. This is the approach that we refer to as the "consultant" model.

1. Action research proceeds at a slower pace than does the consultant approach for reasons made clear by the earlier description of the Wisconsin project. A great deal of time is devoted to discussion, to hearing alternative viewpoints, to reaching consensus, and to the preliminary re-

view and tryout of materials. Under the consultant model, on the other hand, the outside evaluator is expected simply to make the decisions about what is to be done and then to go ahead and do it!

This slower pace may be either a strength or a weakness of action research, depending on circumstances of the evaluation. If one needs to have an evaluation conducted quickly, the consultant model will be preferred. If one would like to proceed at a slower pace in order, for example, to reduce the anxiety often precipitated by an evaluation blitzkrieg, then the action-research model might be preferred.

2. An action-research program will not run by itself. The diffused decision-making function should not be translated into laissez-faire management. It is clear in the consultant model that the evaluation is run by the consultant. The consultant is the expert who decides what is to be done and how it will be done. In the action-research model there is no counterpart to the evaluation consultant; decision making is deliberately shared. Nonetheless, an action-research effort needs some person or agency that will serve the management function (let us call the person or agency simply "the manager"). The manager does not decide what evaluation will be undertaken but does make sure that a decision gets made. Program personnel may determine a schedule for completing the evaluation, but the evaluation manager will worry about getting the resources to meet the schedule.

This manager should also be able to provide program personnel with background information about areas to be evaluated, with assistance in analyzing data, and with help in avoiding common pitfalls in interpreting research results. In fact, the manager should have all of the qualifications of an evaluation consultant—but should not act like one. This is a novel and sometimes difficult role for an evaluation expert to play; there are probably substantial differences among individuals as to how well they can play this role.

3. Taking immediate action based on evaluation results seems more likely to happen with the action-research approach than with the consultant approach. Nonutilization of results produced by an outside evaluator is a notorious problem in educational research, as pointed out in Buhl and Lindquist's introductory chapter and earlier in the present chapter. However, action based on results generated by action research seems to occur readily. In fact—and this is a very interesting point—action is often taken before the results of a particular study are formally reported. In the process of helping to design the evaluation of a program or in helping to collect data, program personnel seem to develop sufficient insight into or information about the problem so that they can begin to take corrective action. Often, a final report based on all of the data, with formal statistical analysis, appropriate editing, and so on, will not be issued until several months *after* corrective action has been initiated.

This situation, as desirable as it may be from the viewpoint of research utilization, creates two special difficulties for the evaluator managing the action-research effort. First, the unveiling of the researcher's marvelous reports is often greeted with the observation, "But those conclusions are no longer valid—we already changed that part of the program." The more effective the project manager is in precipitating participant involvement and immediate use of results, the more the manager appears to be superfluous and perhaps even obtuse. Hence, the second difficulty: the manager's ego gets very little nurturing.

4. The action-research approach is more appropriate for formative evaluation than for summative evaluation. As defined by Bloom, Hastings, and Madaus (1971), summative evaluation relates to end products, certification, accomplishing ultimate goals, and such things, whereas formative evaluation relates to processes, methods used to accomplish goals, intermediate stages of progress, and so on.

With action research, when participants are intimately involved in designing the evaluation, it appears that summative evaluation is too threatening to allow for decisive action. When summative evaluation is needed, it is probably preferable to use the consultant model, especially since disinterestedness is more likely to be important in a summative evaluation such as certification.

In contrast, when formative evaluation is the primary concern—in other words, how to change the program, modify this or that approach, get a new slant on how the program might develop—then action research is more appropriate. Program personnel have a knowledge of the inner workings of their program and of the questions they need answered about those inner workings that would forever escape the attention of the outside evaluator. This point is worth pursuing. When the question of program evaluation first is raised, attention seems to focus most readily on questions calling for summative evaluation. Especially when a program is new, however, the questions of real interest to program personnel are most often those that call for formative evaluation. Thus, participants in action research must be reminded that the evaluation is intended to answer the questions that are of real interest to *them*, not just those questions (often the summative ones) that interest other people.

5. Personalities tend to play a larger role in the action-research approach than in the consultant approach. One could easily surmise this to be the case from the description of the Wisconsin project provided earlier. Action research requires a great deal of personal interaction and if the personalities involved have difficulty relating harmoniously—as, obviously, sometimes happens—then the evaluation effort will be largely unproductive as well as unpleasant. In the consultant model, the interplay of personalities is deliberately minimized. It is an antiseptic approach; even if the principal parties involved are not very compatible, it should make

little difference. In fact, this is a major strength of the consultant model (Scriven, 1975).

How serious a problem is this for action research? In particular circumstances, the entire evaluation effort might be scuttled. One should probably not launch an action-research project if there is reason to anticipate serious personality clashes. To say that "we'll work things out" is probably naive. Persistent interpersonal difficulties are among the most difficult problems in the world to "work out." However, if one finds oneself in the midst of an action-research project and personality differences emerge, a possible remedy is to *get more people involved* in order to provide buffers.

Of course, the interplay of personalities in the action-research approach should not be portrayed exclusively as a source of problems. In Alkin, Daillak, and White's (1979) description of case studies where evaluation seems to have been effective, it appears that, at least often, a cordial personal relationship between project personnel and evaluation personnel—even the development of friendships—may have played a key role in leading to utilization of evaluation results.

References

Alkin, M. C., Daillak, R., and White, P. *Using Evaluations: Does Evaluation Make a Difference?* Beverly Hills, Calif.: Sage, 1979.

Braskamp, L. A., and Brown, R. D. (Eds.) *New Directions for Program Evaluation: Utilization of Evaluative Information.* San Francisco: Jossey-Bass, 1980.

Bloom, B. S., Hastings, J. T., and Madaus, G. *Handbook on Formative and Summative Evaluation of Student Learning.* New York: McGraw-Hill, 1971.

Dressel, P. L. (Ed.). *New Directions for Institutional Research: The Autonomy of Public Colleges.* San Francisco: Jossey-Bass, 1980.

House, E. R. "Assumptions Underlying Evaluation Models." *Educational Researcher,* 1978, 7 (3), 4–12.

Howe, H. "Education Research—The Promise and the Problem." *Educational Researcher,* 1976, 5 (6), 2–7.

Kaiser, R., Mishler, C., and Hogan, T. "Priorities for Evaluation of Nontraditional Degree Programs." *Alternative Higher Education,* in press.

Popham, J. W., and Carlson, D. "Deep Dark Deficits of the Adversary Evaluation Model." *Educational Researcher,* 1977, 6 (6), 3–6.

Scriven, M. J. *Evaluation Bias and Its Control.* Occasional Paper Series, No. 4. Kalamazoo, Mich.: Evaluation Center, Western Michigan University, 1975.

Stake, R. E. *Evaluating Educational Programmes: The Need and the Response.* Paris: Organization for Economic Cooperation and Development, 1976.

Thurston, P. "Revitalizing Adversary Evaluation: Deep Dark Deficits or Muddled Mistaken Musings." *Educational Researcher,* 1978, 7 (7), 3–8.

Thomas P. Hogan is codirector of the Wisconsin Assessment Center, director of the Educational Testing Center, and a faculty member in the education and psychology departments at the University of Wisconsin/Green Bay. He served as principal investigator of the evaluation project described in this chapter.

*One person's research channeled to one institutional
leader, even the president, is less likely to get used
than many perspectives flowing through various
committees, offices, and individuals.*

Multiple Perspectives, Multiple Channels

Ernest G. Palola

Action research confronts two contexts of awesome complexity: learning
and organizational decision making. Buhl and Lindquist address this
challenge in Chapter One. In this chapter I wish to stress that simple
evaluations of learning, and simple routes for getting those evaluations
used in one's college, just will not work. In building an effective (meaning
that it *has effect*) institutional research operation, I have found that a key to
that effectiveness lies in "multiple perspectives, multiple channels." In
other words, one must study learning from various angles if it is to be seen
clearly and if findings are to be trusted. And one must disseminate findings
various ways through various organizational routes if decision-makers are
to be stimulated toward action.

The multiple perspectives, multiple channels approach that my
colleagues and I have developed for Empire State College and several other
colleges is called PERC (Program Effectiveness and Related Costs). In this
chapter, I will briefly review that evaluation model, outline the ways we get
its data used, and conclude with several principles for research use that we
have found especially helpful.

PERC

This section briefly describes the PERC framework. PERC takes
seriously the problem of integrating effectiveness and cost efforts into a

J. Lindquist (Ed.), *New Directions for Institutional Research: Increasing the
Utilization of Institutional Research*, no. 32. San Francisco: Jossey-Bass, December 1981.

coherent, powerful, and integrated package that can be adapted to any undergraduate teaching institution. Although I will address this model in particular, other evaluation strategies that incorporate multiple perspectives also should provide the richness of data needed to breed the decision-maker's trust in them.

Weaknesses in available studies led to the development of an evaluation strategy that focuses on the master question: *What kinds of students working with what kinds of faculty in what kinds of learning programs in what ways at what cost accomplish what learning outcomes?* Figure 1 illustrates the interconnectedness of each of these variables. Let us examine two of these components—learning outcomes and costs—more closely before we look at how PERC works.

Learning Outcomes. The first component of this framework is outcomes. Each college should identify its own set of outcomes appropriate to the kinds of students it attracts and the kinds of educational programs it offers. Colleges should specify what their students are trying to attain, what the college is trying to achieve, and what kinds of learning programs will produce these outcomes. In individualized education programs, for example, we start by defining outcomes based on individual student needs and objectives. Each student designs a degree program that provides the basis for measuring outcomes. The degree program is the individual program of the student. It includes prior learning and contract learning, with the appropriate mix of concentration and general learning. It is the basic planning document for the student's work and for action research.

The PERC framework classifies individual student objectives into eight outcome categories. These categories are substantive knowledge, communication skills, cognitive development, personal, occupational, public service, and unanticipated outcomes. To illustrate, substantive knowledge is the level of competence achieved within the context of a student's goals; cognitive outcomes include comprehension, analysis, evaluation, synthesis, and application; and developmental outcomes cover interpersonal competence, awareness, clarification of purposes, self-understanding, and self-consistency. The idea is to create a classification of outcomes that is comprehensive and includes most key dimensions across different institutional types. The classification thereby offers various decision-makers a range of data pertinent to their particular concerns.

Learning Costs. There are essential features of the PERC cost framework that differ from other cost systems. First, it has been developed to supplement the educational effectiveness framework: cost data is developed around and reported in relation to the educational effectiveness measures. Several audiences are interested mainly in what education costs, not in its quality. We believe, however, that how much learning for the

Figure 1. The Five Elements of PERC

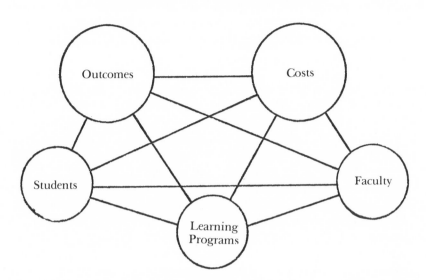

dollar is the bottom line. The quality of education, in terms of "real learning," is what makes it worth the money.

The second distinguishing characteristic of the PERC cost framework is that it is triggered by the individual student's learning experiences rather than by some budgetary formula (for example, full-time equivalent (FTE) students or credit hours). Third, the framework requires the inclusion of certain costs that are optional or missing in other systems (for example, in-kind contributions of services, facilities, materials, and programs). Fourth, PERC treats the cost of locations, learning resources, and programs as deferred assets. Fifth, portions of faculty salaries devoted to administration are assigned as overhead, not as direct instructional cost. Average salaries are calculated across organizational units of an institution in order to minimize peculiarities in age, rank, and salary of staff in a given location or program.

Although the PERC framework differs from other cost systems in the above ways, the framework has been constructed so that reports may be comparable with most other cost frameworks, including the major efforts of the National Center for Higher Education Management Systems (NCHEMS—See Debus, 1974, and Palola and Green, 1980). By summing the appropriate individual student costs developed through PERC, reports can be based on more conventional cost analysis units: FTE, credit hours, major, and so on.

Multiple Perspectives. Many studies use a single type and source of data—for example, standardized tests to measure student learning. Research on complex programs such as student learning and on the link between programs and learning belies unidimensional or single-perspective research. In addition, conclusions from such one-sided research are less trusted by institutional leaders than those derived from a variety of measures. The multiple perspectives strategy developed for the PERC framework, in contrast, rests on five components: multiple *observers* of student learning, multiple *methods* of assessing student learning, multiple *standards* for evaluating student learning, multiple *decison-makers* utilizing data relevant to policy questions, and multiple *time periods* for measuring change in student learning.

The multiple perspectives strategy is shown in Figure 2. It contains three key ideas: first, student learning is the focus of program evaluation—thus its placement at the center of the figure. Second, several observers make judgments of student learning utilizing various ways of knowing and ways of evaluating. This array of observers and methods to detect student learning and growth is critical to the pluralistic idea of evaluation. Finally, an independent or neutral research and evaluation staff synthesizes the data and prepares policy-oriented reports for different decision-makers.

Let us consider in more detail the various parts of the multiple perspectives strategy shown in Figure 2. PERC conceptualizes the process of learning and teaching as complex, interactive, and unique but also as patterned. For example, students are the primary consumers of this process and are in an especially advantageous position to evaluate certain aspects of their own learning. They, as observers, have a strong interest in assessing their own learning in terms of standards contained in their objectives for learning. Thus, students may evaluate their own learning on certain outcomes, such as subject matter knowledge, communication skills, or interpersonal competence. Correspondingly, faculty, as observers, can also evaluate students on the same outcomes and provide another, more detached and more formally expert, perspective on what students have or have not learned. As a result of this double perspective, we expect to find some agreement on outcomes (especially cognitive ones) but also some differences in outcome judgments (especially in the developmental domain). Relatively few studies have been conducted that apply a multiple perspectives strategy wherein several observers provide independent evaluations of a given student's learning and growth (see Wilson and others, 1975).

Other observers of learning outcomes as shown in Figure 2 are the research office, the administration, and outside evaluators such as accreditors. The research staff that uses PERC may conduct its own evaluation of student learning (for example, with standardized tests to measure student mastery of subject-matter knowledge or cognitive and affective growth) as well as provide the focal points for carrying out the PERC framework. In this capacity, the research staff has the responsibility to bring together data

Figure 2. PERC'S Multiple Perspectives Strategy

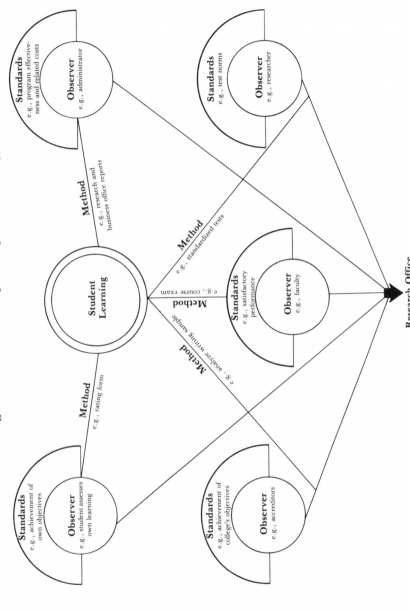

Standards
e.g., program effective-
ness and related costs

Observer
e.g., administrator

Standards
e.g., test norms

Observer
e.g., researcher

Standards
e.g., achievement of
own objectives

Observer
e.g., student assesses
own learning

Standards
e.g., achievement of
college's objectives

Observer
e.g., accreditors

**Student
Learning**

Standards
e.g., satisfactory
performance

Observer
e.g., faculty

Method
e.g., research and
business office reports

Method
e.g., standardized tests

Method
e.g., course exam

Method
e.g., analyze writing sample

Method
e.g., rating form

Research Office

Synthesizes data and prepares reports for different *Decision-Makers*
e.g., students, faculty, administrators, accreditors, parents, state officials, national agencies

provided by several observers, to analyze the data, and to prepare reports that can be of use to different decision-makers.

Administrators and observers outside the college look at student learning from a different vantage point. Generally, they are removed from direct participation in the learning/teaching process, but they may periodically interview students and faculty to question how learning is occurring. College administrators rely upon research and business reports as the primary source of information from which they can judge program effectiveness and related costs. Observers outside the college, such as accreditors, state officials, national agencies, and so on, examine the question of student learning in terms of the college's objectives and certain performance standards held by accrediting agencies or governmental bodies. For example, accreditors (through the institutional self-study process) investigate the conditions of education at a given college and provide an evaluation of student learning in the context of overall college operations.

Comparability. The question of comparability has been a key topic in higher education research for years, and pressures have led on occasion to highly questionable comparisons. Does an evaluation system such as PERC allow cross-institutional comparisons? Our view is that PERC can be used in this way but that its primary focus is to develop good and useful *intra*institutional data for all types of learning programs. This is challenge enough for now. As time goes on and experience with PERC grows, a strong base for interinstitutional comparisons will emerge. At present, interinstitutional studies must be done carefully because comparative data is not necessarily identical. Students, faculty, and programs exist in various sizes, shapes, structures, climates, and so on. Some definitions are nearly universal and transfer well, such as sex, age, SAT scores. Others, however, do not transfer well—for instance, student types, "full-time" faculty, and so on. As difficult as comparative research is, additional efforts should be made to find ways in which PERC can speak to the questions and issues of cross-institutional comparisons.

To sum up, student learning and growth is a complex process, so reliance on a single observer, a single method of data collection, or a single standard of evaluation is inadequate in assessing learning outcomes. The strongest way to generate credible data about learning is a multiple perspectives strategy that requires several observers of student learning, several methods of data collection regarding that learning, and several standards of judgment to determine the effectiveness of that learning. This strategy has important consequences for data management. For example, working with survey questionnaire data is one thing; working with interviews or documents is something else. And the opportunity to link programs to outcomes is much different when researchers have several kinds (rather than one kind) of data.

Multiple Channels. We have found highly useful five kinds of research reports and several interpersonal channels for communicating those reports. Figure 3 summarizes the report formats.

Bullets are short, targeted responses to institutional questions. They usually contain one or two tables and a few paragraphs explaining how the data relate to a particular institutional concern. For audiences (faculty and trustees, for instance) who will read short, snappy summaries on learning but have neither the time nor inclination for longer reports, bullets are invaluable. Also, they can be used to target specific information to specific groups, such as a profile of female students to a committee on the college's responsiveness to women. A second type consists of *occasional papers* that relate to the PERC framework. These background papers concentrate on a particular topic, like faculty workload, program costs, or educational outcomes in an effort to provide information for local consumption. *Research reports,* the third type, are longer than bullets and occasional papers; they provide thorough discussion of a research study. For example, an early research report, *Success After Graduation* (Lehmann, 1974), summarized findings of the first administration of PERC's Graduate Follow-Up Questionnaire (GFO). A fourth type of report is the *monograph,* which introduces general research, theory, and practice in an extensive discussion of educational issues. *The Empire State College Mentor: An Emerging Role* (Bradley, 1975), for example, presented interview and questionnaire findings in the context of a national movement of higher education toward individualized education concepts. *Handbooks* such as the *PERC Handbook* (Palola and others, 1976) are the fifth type of research report in the series. This type of report is printed to facilitate use—in a common binder, with wide margins, illustrations, references to alternate methods—and presents step-by-step procedures and techniques, including samples of questionnaires, interview schedules, rating forms, and the like, used to analyze particular institutional policy matters.

Written reports are not the only format for delivering data. If local conditions make it possible, it is also useful to have research staff members who belong to, and can report to, such various institutional bodies as the administrative cabinet, faculty senate, planning task forces, and faculty committees. Or the research staff can meet with groups of faculty or administrators (that is, with a department) to exchange ideas on a given data set. Often, for such sessions, the presentation can be tailored to meet the particular needs of the faculty or administrative group. We find that unless we balance time in research with time actively engaged with college decision-makers, research time is wasted.

Involving Leaders in Research. Besides our getting out into the institution, we need to involve institutional leaders with us so that the research becomes theirs as well as ours. To facilitate this involvement, we recommend that the research process involve a variety of people and groups

Figure 3. PERC Report Types

Bullets	*Occasional Papers*
• Primarily informational • Short: table and a few paragraphs • Restricted distribution • Targeted to particular questions • Single dimension	• Single dimension • Up to 15 pages • May have wide audience

Research Reports	*Monographs*

• In-depth reports on particular
  research questions
• Often contain policy recom-
  mendations
• Fifteen pages and up, local
  audience
	• Relate to broad policy questions
	• Wide audience
	• Often lengthy
	• Relate to literature base
	• Reviewed widely before
	  distribution

Handbooks

• Methodologically oriented
• Wide audience
• May be related to literature base
• Reviewed widely before distribution

at all the action-research stages outlined by Buhl and Lindquist in Chapter One: defining the research problems and the policy areas to examine, deciding on data-collection strategies and techniques, analyzing and interpreting the findings, and using the data in policy making.

An institution-wide advisory group, including faculty, administrators, and students, may counsel the research office on virtually every aspect of its operations. For example, the advisory group may help make general plans, design projects, develop schedules, revise research instruments, review reports, and disseminate results. It also provides a convenient source of information for faculty and others at various locations of the institution about research office activities. Informally, then, the advisory group may function as an institution-wide extension of the research staff, and in this capacity it can solicit and answer questions and communicate ideas. Overall, the advisory group may contribute significantly to the research effort in making findings more meaningful, timely, and pertinent to an institution.

Others whose ideas are regularly sought include such administrative groups as the president's cabinet and council of deans. Cabinets normally consist of the president and the vice-presidents. The research office should have membership on and thus direct input into executive deliberations. The cabinet is a major policy advisory body. Its knowledge of and contributions to evaluation activities are essential to the success of the research effort. Usually, a high percentage of specific research tasks are generated by a cabinet, which then uses the findings. A council of deans often consists of the cabinet members plus deans, directors, and other administrators. This group may also generate and receive various reports, and its views may shape activities.

In addition to the above sources of input and advice, the research office can maintain liaison with the faculty senate and long-range planning committees. Most educational institutions have a planning group with primary responsibility for the coordination of study groups and task forces examining various planning issues. This group often plays a major role in long-range planning and priority setting. At various times, the research office with PERC-like data may provide useful and pertinent information for long-range planning processes.

Although widespread involvement by various administrative offices, senate committees, and other groups is important to research office work and to the development and utilization of program evaluations, it is essential that the research office maintain a working balance with these groups. All views must be considered in designing and implementing a system such as PERC; simultaneously, measures should be taken to develop some degree of independence from the pressures, demands, and necessities of line administrative activities.

Protecting Privacy. Confidentiality is a critical issue in research use. Because of the longitudinal nature of an evaluation process such as PERC, it is necessary that the individual student's privacy be maintained. As PERC is designed, participating students receive three different questionnaires throughout their undergraduate work and at least one follow-up questionnaire some time after graduation. Information on confidentiality is printed in all questionnaires, and research staff members respond to questions and comments on this subject. No student's identity is displayed in oral or written reports. Data on faculty are similarly anonymous. Although this tight rein on confidentiality can also inhibit open access of interested decision-makers to data, we find that, in the long run, it breeds trust in our ethics and that, in turn, increases trust in our honest portrayal of the evidence.

Emerging Principles

The aim of this chapter has been to demonstrate how the PERC system handles problems of data use and dissemination. While working with our research team, Jack Lindquist identified at least eight general principles and several specific examples validated by the literature and our past efforts. The following paragraphs define those principles.

Involve Users Throughout. Our experiences, and extensive earlier evidence regarding research utilization, confirm that people do not respond favorably to research questions, administration, analysis, and conclusions conducted without their involvement. Involvement breeds ownership, stimulates credibility, and interest. One specific technique already mentioned is to establish a *research advisory committee* composed of faculty members, administrators, and students interested in research and respected by their peers. Second, meet with the academic and administrative units at each stage of the study to share data and receive feedback. Third, hold workshops and assist the committees or task forces in studying the data further or pursuing the problems suggested by the data. Fourth, involve students throughout the study since they are closest to learning experiences. Think of the whole process as a continuous reciprocal exchange between researchers and those who can benefit by the information.

Get to the Powerful. Some people have more power than others to block or accomplish data use. Some people with influence are more open to data about costs or educational effectiveness than others. Learn who they are and establish personal interchange with them regarding the whole study. Keep Kurt Lewin's lesson in mind: don't just build support; focus especially on reducing resistance. The key influential people are likely to be executive administrators plus senior professors with strong professional credentials or high governance positions.

Fit Data to Interests. People learn best what they are motivated to learn, what they feel a need to know. By interviewing campus members, sitting in committees, and holding workshops designed to clarify institutional goals and problems, one can link program-effectiveness data to expressed concerns. The need for information may precede the information, but need may also be sparked by data. A good strategy is to search out information needs before data-based workshops are held and then to request committee or individual time to share unsolicited yet potentially important information that might clarify or heighten a need.

Fit Data to Learning Styles. Faculty, like students, learn best experientially, or by reading prose, or by examining numbers; quickly or slowly; by themselves or in groups; inductively or deductively. Clearly, *one* dissemination approach is not adequate for everyone. Attempt to vary approaches for various users, include something for everyone—quotations or cases for humanists, creative products for artists, numbers and hypotheses for scientists, demonstration exercises for experientialists, and quick summaries for busy faculty and administrators.

Underwhelm. Social science data, especially for those who are not social scientists, can be tedious even if imaginatively presented. Only a few points will be remembered from one interaction, with little likelihood that the user will pore over the data later. Either give out only the most relevant data for the occasion or help the group (or individual) during your interaction pare down the information to a few important points for action.

Seek Small Cross-Group or One-to-One Interactions. Research indicates that only persons ready to agree with a message are likely to be persuaded by formal communications—written reports and speeches, in this case (Rogers and Shoemaker, 1971). Others need personal interaction with message senders and with opinion leaders. Large faculty meetings or meetings of only one reference group (for instance all administrators) are not likely to result in more than the confirmation of data supporting the views of major speakers plus an attack on contrary information (lousy sample, biased or ambiguous question, irrelevant point). The best way to keep people focused on and openly evaluating the data is to have trained leaders help small groups with mixed membership (students, social scientists, humanists, administrators, liberals, conservatives) as they work through the data. Or work one-on-one with the major influential people. Asking small groups to identify major institutional strengths as well as problems suggested by the data, then having them report back to the general group, serves not only to free discussion but to lend a sense of reliability and validity to problems several groups independently identify. Chapter Five (Terrass and Pomrenke) elaborates the importance of these "change agent" tactics and skills.

Encourage Follow-Up Structures. We have all read interesting institutional research reports or have attended stimulating campus workshops but then have done nothing to follow up on the issues raised. To get data used after initial scrutiny, you must devise some follow-up structure. The least formal is an individual's commitment to do something in his or her own teaching, learning, or administrative practices. It helps if these individuals make that commitment with someone else so there is some external stimulus for follow through. It also helps if the institution provides time, training, and funds to aid the individual in the complex business of attempting something new. A more formal follow-up structure might be an administrator's or governance chairperson's commitment to putting an issue on a governance agenda. Stronger is the establishment of a special task force whose job will be to coordinate follow through, to see that the institution responds to the issues generally agreed upon. Or a task force may take up a specific problem. Staff assistance, released time, and budget can make the difference between feeble attempts and important institutional improvements in cost-effectiveness.

Provide Contract Assistance After Initial Dissemination. Neither campus users nor researchers and follow-up helpers want to spend much time disseminating research findings if this dissemination is not reciprocated in research use. The research advisory committee at Empire State College decided that the negotiated contract be extended from the initial use with students and with collective bargaining to include research dissemination and use. Researchers and utilization specialists will now put in time and effort only if interested faculty, student, or administrative groups agree to put substantial time and effort into examining and following up the data. The parties sign a Research Dissemination and Use Contract.

Study Your Own Data Dissemination and Use. One of the assignments of Empire State College's research associate for policy analysis was to study dissemination and use of cost-effectiveness data to learn what works and why. In this way, general knowledge utilization strategies can be tested and adjusted to fit local circumstances.

Case Studies

Some of the above principles are illustrated in the following cases of evaluation and the use of data in decision making. In each case, a program serving the particular needs of learners or serving an institutional academic policy is the focus.

Evaluation of a Minorities Outreach Program. The first case is especially good at demonstrating how the effective planning of evaluation activities can facilitate understanding and communication throughout the evaluation itself. It illustrates the importance of involving users, of linking to influential people, and of fitting data to diverse interests. A special unit of Empire State College was created in Brooklyn, New York, to serve the needs of local black citizens. This unit began in 1974 with a major private foundation grant, and, at the end of the three years, an extensive evaluation study was undertaken to determine the effectiveness of the program in meeting its goals and objectives. The multiperspective strategy of PERC was especially appropriate to this evaluation since this unit served multiple constituencies—the sponsoring foundation, the college, the college's New York City center, the Brooklyn community, and the students themselves. A great deal of time and patience was used to ensure that representatives of these five different constituencies had input into the evaluation plan. Before the evaluation took place, meetings occurred involving these constituencies and members of the research staff. An evaluation plan was eventually written that included the evaluation objectives, ways to obtain data from each constituency, the variety of instruments and data sources to be tapped, and the general content planned for the evaluation.

These preparations not only cleared the air on what the evaluation was to include and exclude but also set the stage for interviews and questionnaires. Since the various parties knew what was coming and had contributed to and supported the evaluation plan, they cooperated fully and freely in providing data during the data collection phase. Based on this preparation and evaluation work, dissemination and use of results occurred quite smoothly. A final report was submitted to the funding source to fulfill certain requirements of the grant, and discussions occurred at several levels within the college to secure state-supported positions, facilities, and office supplies.

Due to time pressures (that's reality!), we were not able to involve users during the data analysis to the extent desired. It was possible, however, to get some preliminary reaction and feedback as various sections of the report were being written. This proved useful and avoided, at least in one instance, drawing faulty conclusions from sketchy data. This procedure also eliminated surprises and created more confidence in conclusions.

Feedback on Student Attrition. In a second case, we see more clearly the operation of the principles of underwhelming the audience, providing contract assistance, and encouraging follow-up. This second case focuses on an issue of continuing interest to academic administrators—student attrition. When enrollment projections are a bit off, administrators become keenly aware of any losses within the existing student-body, and they especially seek policy improvements that may reduce attrition.

In this case, the research office was asked to prepare an "attrition study." An overly zealous effort on the part of a few members of the research staff resulted in a "Cadillac" research design. At the end of the data collection period, enough computer printouts existed to paper several rooms; charts and tables were made to tell the story every which way; and even the term *attrition* was said to have at least six different meanings. An astute senior researcher knew that "underwhelm" was the way to present the attrition study to busy administrators. A *much* simplified summary of findings was presented to them with the understanding that more details, breakdowns, charts, and graphs were available. As it turned out, two vice-presidents did ask for and receive more details at a subsequent meeting with members of the research staff.

This case had one other interesting outcome—follow-up meetings with deans who then volunteered to collect detailed data on their own programs to compare with and elaborate on research office figures. This additional data gathering also led to a series of steps to combat attrition. Simple measures such as calling students who recently withdrew not only improved relations with students but also netted a few re-enrollees. Furthermore, meetings were scheduled among other administrators across the college to pool information, data interpretations, and conclusions and to discuss specific ways to reduce student attrition.

Summary

This chapter attempts to show the use and importance of multiple perspectives and multiple channels in the dissemination of research data. Common sense tells us that it is important to let people know what's happening, why certain data are being collected, who will receive research findings, and how program evaluation can potentially improve program effectiveness. What is not so obvious is how to find enough time and skill to do what we know must be done. One thing that will help is to talk about the principles of dissemination and data use at the very beginning of each evaluation project and to convince key persons of the value and importance of following these principles.

These dissemination and use strategies are based on extensive prior research and action. User ownership, linkage to influential people, personal interaction, fitting dissemination to user learning styles and interests, establishing follow-up structures, and studying the whole process are principles we followed at Empire State College, and we recommend their application in other institutional settings.

References

Bradley, A. P., Jr. *The Empire State College Mentor: An Emerging Role.* Saratoga Spring, N.Y.: Empire State College Research Series, 1975.

Debus, R. *Detailed Analysis of Empire State College Effectiveness Program and Relationship to NCHEMS Program.* Saratoga Springs, N.Y.: Office of Research and Evaluation, Empire State College, 1974.

Lehmann, T. *Success After Graduation.* Saratoga Springs, N.Y.: Empire State College Research Series, 1974.

Palola, E., Lehmann, T., Bradley, A. P., and Debus, R. *PERC Handbook.* Saratoga Springs, N.Y.: Empire State College Research Series, 1976.

Palola, E., Lehmann, T., and Sunshine, M. *The Methodology of PERC.* Saratoga Springs, N.Y.: Empire State College Research Series, 1977.

Palola, E., Sunshine, M., and Lehmann, T. *The Uses of PERC.* Saratoga Springs, N.Y.: Empire State College Research Series, 1977.

Palola, E., and Green, D. *Linking Outcomes and Costs: New Strategies for Institutional Management.* Saratoga Springs, N.Y.: Empire State College Research Series, 1980.

Rogers, E., and Shoemaker, F. F. *Communication of Innovations.* New York: Free Press, 1971.

Wilson, R. C., Gaff, J. G., and others. *College Professors and Their Impact on Students.* New York: Wiley, 1975.

Ernest G. Palola has been conducting research on the social organization of higher education for twenty years and has published works on individualized education, learning outcomes, educational and organizational evaluation, stress management, and national planning. He organized the Office of Research and Evaluation at Empire State College, an institution recognized for innovative approaches to learning services for adults. Currently he is organizing a research institute that will conduct studies on several themes important to professional/client relationships in adult development.

*Useful data on the outcomes of general education are
hard to come by, but when they can be generated in
ways that are credible to decision-makers and
comparable with results at other institutions, the
impact can be considerable.*

Outcome Evaluation for Revitalizing General Education

Aubrey Forrest

It has now been several years since the Carnegie Foundation for the
Advancement of Teaching issued its report stating:

> General education is now a disaster area. It has been on the defensive
> and losing ground for more than 100 years. It represents the accre-
> tions of history more than a thoughtful concern for specialized
> current needs . . . . If colleges cannot define what they intend to
> accomplish in general education, cannot specifically describe how
> it will benefit students who engage in it, and cannot deliver an effec-
> tive general education component, they should seriously consider
> eliminating it entirely.

General education is still a concern in most American colleges and universities. Many of the consumers and supporters of higher education continue
to question seriously the effectiveness of general education programs.
Many institutions question whether anyone can really measure such effectiveness. Some question whether such information, even if available,
would really have much impact on improving general education or on the

J. Lindquist (Ed.), *New Directions for Institutional Research: Increasing the
Utilization of Institutional Research*, no. 32. San Francisco: Jossey-Bass, December 1981.

degree of support received for such programs. Is there a way not only to generate sound data on general education outcomes but also to get the data used?

Finding satisfactory answers to this question is the task set for the College Outcome Measures Project (COMP). COMP was organized by the American College Testing Program (ACT) in 1976, as a response to the growing need for assessment instruments and procedures to measure and evaluate certain kinds of knowledge and skills that undergraduates are expected to acquire as a result of general education—the knowledge and skills that are believed necessary for effective functioning in adult society. (Descriptive materials about COMP may be obtained by writing to ACT in Iowa City, Iowa.)

The outcomes identified in COMP are:

1. *Communicating:* The student can send and receive information in a variety of modes (written, graphic, oral, numeric, and symbolic), within a variety of settings (one-to-one, in small and large groups), and for a variety of purposes (for example, to inform, to understand, to persuade, and to analyze).

2. *Solving Problems:* The student can analyze a variety of problems (for example, scientific, social, personal), can select or create solutions to problems, and can implement solutions.

3. *Clarifying Values:* The student can identify his or her personal values and the personal values of other individuals, can understand how personal values develop, and can analyze the implications of decisions made on the basis of personally held values.

4. *Functioning within Social Institutions:* The student can identify those activities and institutions that constitute the social aspects of a culture (for example, governmental and economic systems, religion, marital and familial institutions, employment, and civic volunteer and recreational organizations). The student understands the impact that social institutions have on individuals in a culture and can analyze his or her own and others' personal functioning within social institutions.

5. *Using Science and Technology:* The student can identify those activities and products that constitute the scientific or technological aspects of a culture (for example, transportation, housing, energy, processed food, clothing, health maintenance, entertainment and recreation, mood-altering methods, national defense, communication, and data processing), can understand the impact of such activities and products on the individuals and the physical environment in a culture, and can analyze the uses of technological products in a culture and his or her personal use of such products.

6. *Using the Arts:* The student can identify those activities and products that constitute the artistic aspects of a culture (for example, graphic art, music, drama, literature, dance, sculpture, film, architecture);

can understand the impact that art, in its various forms, has on individuals in a culture; and can analyze uses of works of art within a culture and his or her personal use of art.

To date, ACT has been assisted in this experimental program by about 150 postsecondary institutions and agencies and by an advisory/ evaluation panel composed of distinguished educators. A key feature of COMP's continuing research and development effort is the substantial assistance provided by faculty and administrators at participating institutions and agencies. These people have been especially helpful in identifying the desired educational outcomes, in developing COMP materials, and in trying out the assessment instruments by administering them to college students and to effectively functioning adults not enrolled in college. This involvement is akin to that described and advocated by Tom Hogan in Chapter Two.

COMP Cases

It is still too early in the project to have addressed satisfactorily all the issues raised above. However, case studies of participating institutions are suggestive of some emerging conclusions. Many institutions are finding these tentative conclusions useful to consider as they grapple with the problems of revitalizing general education programs. One major conclusion emerging from COMP is that information about the effectiveness of general education programs *can* be obtained and that this information *can* lead to the improvement of the programs as well as help to maintain support for them. There are instances, reported informally to ACT by institutions participating in COMP, in which information about the effectiveness of a general education program has been important in making critical decisions. These reports indicate the use of COMP data, but the results could be obtained from other, reasonably equivalent, evidence of learning outcomes. We have not been able to document directly all of these reports, nor would we necessarily recommend that other institutions emulate the course of action selected by a given institution. However, the examples related here do serve to illustrate how evaluation information can be of practical significance.

Assessing Innovative General Education. In the review of initial regional accreditation of a highly innovative and new college, accreditors raised the issue of the level of performance by the graduates in general knowledge and skill areas. Although the institution had developed a nontraditional program, it did claim objectives and standards commonly stated by more traditional and long-established liberal arts institutions. By testing a representative sample of graduating seniors with COMP instruments and by making comparisons with normative data compiled on graduating seniors at more traditional institutions, the college was able to convince the review team that the general knowledge and skill level of graduates from its program were at least equivalent to that of graduates from other, accredited institutions. This was considered an important piece of evidence that led to full accreditation, which in turn should help to make the job of fund raising and student recruitment more effective.

Evaluating Standards for External Degrees. In a state that had established an external degree program for adults that involved several public universities, faculty and legislators were raising questions as to the standards for degree granting. The main question was whether or not graduates of the external degree program were as competent in general knowledge and skill areas as those who graduated from residential or on-campus programs. By testing a representative sample of recent graduates from the external degree program and by comparing the group results with the national norms developed in COMP, the coordinators of the program at the state level were able to successfully defend the program as having appropriate quality control. This important piece of evidence led to continued support for the program.

Satisfying External Judges. In a state where there was a desire to direct funds into programs that could be demonstrated to be effective, a public university was successful in obtaining additional state funding because it could document, through testing a representative sample of seniors, that its graduates were leaving with a high level of general knowledge and skill in comparison with COMP national norms.

Because a private college had established a continuous evaluation program of its general education component, using COMP instruments and procedures, the college could document the degree of effectiveness of various elements in the component. The college sought to make improvements where appropriate, but these improvements required some additional funding. The fact that the continuous evaluation program was in existence at the college was an important factor in the decision of a private foundation to grant the money needed for curricular experimentation, reported the funder.

In a professional undergraduate program, the students were required to take only a few courses outside of the professional field of study. However, because the professional courses had been designed to be broad in content and to include basic knowledge and skill development, the faculty believed that the general knowledge and skill development of the students had been appropriately attended to. In coming under review for reaccreditation, the professional accrediting body questioned this belief. The administrators of the program were able to successfully defend the program by providing evidence that the graduates were performing on COMP instruments at levels in all areas equivalent to graduates of liberal arts programs at institutions participating in COMP.

A small, private college with a set of core course requirements composing about 40 percent of a student's baccalaureate program was experiencing difficulty in recruiting students. The admissions staff claimed that many prospective students questioned the relevance of what seemed to these students to be a heavy core requirement. After gathering and disseminating information about student gains in important general knowledge and skill areas, the admissions staff reported that what had been perceived by prospective students to be a negative feature (that is, the core requirements) was now being perceived by parents and students as a positive attraction of the college.

The faculty at a university that wanted to increase the enrollment of older adult students experimented with COMP instruments and concluded that the recruitment and advising program was not as effective as it could be in assisting adults in choosing general education courses or in receiving credit for prior learning in general education areas. A decision was made to use COMP instruments to facilitate recruitment and advising.

Satisfying Internal Judges. A university had established a program for awarding credit for prior experiential learning through a process of student portfolio evaluation. The question arose from faculty and adult students as to the appropriateness of the standards being employed, particularly in general education areas. Through the use of COMP instruments and procedures, administrators of the program were able to provide evidence that students awarded credit in general education areas were generally exhibiting abilities in those areas equivalent to graduates of liberal arts programs at institutions participating in COMP.

The faculty of a broadly interdisciplinary graduate program had concluded that existing graduate school admission tests were inappropriate for selecting students for their program. An experimental use of COMP tests led to the conclusion that information from COMP testing would assist the program administrators in selecting candidates more appropriate to the objectives of the program.

Many faculty at a college expressed dissatisfaction with the perceived knowledge and skill levels of graduating seniors. An initial testing, with COMP instruments, of a representative sample of seniors tended to confirm the faculty concerns, at least in some knowledge and skill areas. The test results were considered important evidence to support curricular change. The college now plans to continue testing to verify the effectiveness of curricular changes.

A group of faculty at a university had designed a series of multidisciplinary courses for freshmen and wanted to evaluate the effectiveness of the series. The series was offered to freshmen as an alternative to the traditionally required courses taken by freshmen. The students in the new series and a matched sample drawn from the freshmen taking the normal sequence of courses were tested at the beginning and again at the end of the year in order to make comparisons in gains. Support for the new series was generated by showing that these students made larger gains in performance than those in the traditional sequence.

One college participated in COMP as a part of its faculty development program. The interest at the institution was not only in the information that would be generated about the general education program but the experience with proven alternative forms of measuring student learning that COMP provides. Several faculty reported that they were able to improve their in-course examinations.

A college had developed a competency-based program for older adults as an alternative to its traditional general education program for younger students, and the question of whether to continue the alternative program was raised. A major issue in the decision was the degree to which students in the alternative program were achieving knowledge and skills in comparison to students in the traditional program. Samples of students were drawn from each program and tested using COMP instruments and procedures. Although the two groups performed at generally the same level, some deficiencies in the quality control mechanisms of the nontraditional program were discovered and corrected.

COMP instruments were administered to freshmen and seniors at one institution that did not have stated outcome expectations for its general education program. The institution did have a statement of distribution requirements, but there was neither a clear rationale for deciding what courses would meet the distribution requirements nor any statement of why the distribution requirements existed in the first place. The information gained from the testing procedure helped to clarify the need for a clearly stated rationale; it also greatly assisted faculty in their efforts to articulate the specific expectations in learning outcomes for the general education component.

A public university was faced with a proposal from its governing board to raise admission standards because the board thought that the quality of the graduates was declining to an unacceptable level. The implementation of the standards would have resulted in reduced enrollment at the institution and probably in a reduction in the funding level for the institution. Through the use of data gained through COMP instruments, the institution was able to show that the abilities of the graduating seniors were at an appropriate level by comparing the scores of the seniors with the scores of a group of elite alumni who also took COMP tests. Furthermore, it was shown that the ability levels of entering freshmen were at a level that was appropriate to the educational program of the university.

A college that had abandoned a core curriculum in the 1960s had come to believe that the general abilities of graduates had declined to an unacceptable level. This belief was partially confirmed from COMP test data. Certain course requirements were reinstated in problem areas and an evaluation program of continuous testing was implemented.

The faculty at the university believed that grossly unequal standards were being applied from one section to another in a required course in the general education curriculum as well as among the various required courses of the curriculum. Data from COMP testing confirmed this belief. The university reached the conclusion that all students must pass a common set of examinations in general education in order to graduate.

The administrator of a basic skill development program sought to ensure that it was being as effective as possible. Specifically, the administrator was interested in experimenting with different ways to teach writing and speaking. By establishing a program of continuous pretesting and posttesting of students, the administrator is now able to determine which teaching strategies will work best with which types of students.

A college wishing to monitor continuously the effectiveness of its general education program experimented with COMP tests and learned to develop valid, reliable, and cost-effective instruments in general education areas not covered by COMP instruments. This created a battery of tests that accurately measure student learning in all areas thought by the local faculty to be significant.

A college faculty that was dissatisfied with the problem-solving abilities of its graduating seniors decided to experiment with changing existing courses to focus more on problem-solving exercises. An ongoing use of COMP instruments provides feedback to determine what strategies used in the courses seem to work best in helping students improve problem-solving skills.

Generating Confidence in Outcomes Data

These are but some of the examples from COMP that demonstrate how documentation of the degree of effectiveness can lead to revitalization of general education programs. Many other examples could be cited. But rather than attempt to describe in any greater detail *what* has been the impact on individual institutions and programs in COMP, we feel it is more useful to attempt to describe *why* the impact has occurred. In this way we might learn not only how best to gather data about general education programs but also how best to get decision-makers (administrators, faculty, students, and external audiences) to pay attention to the data during the decision-making process. If the institution is delivering an effective general education component, it should want to attract the support it deserves. If the component has serious weaknesses, the institution should want to make appropriate corrections.

It seems almost axiomatic that the degree to which information about the effectiveness of a general education program will, in fact, have impact on the program depends on the commitment of relevant decision-makers to evaluate the information and to take appropriate action based on the information. Administrators will evaluate the information and decide whether or not to continue, certify, modify, or eliminate a program. Students will evaluate the information and decide whether or not to enroll. Faculty will evaluate the information and decide whether or not curricular changes are in order. Funding sources will evaluate the information and decide whether or not to advance money to the institution. Employers will evaluate the information and decide whether graduates might make good employees. The key question is how to generate this kind of commitment.

This brings us to a second major conclusion emerging from COMP: The amount of commitment to use information in decision making depends, to a large extent, on the degree of confidence decision-makers have in the significance of the information itself and the degree of confidence they have that acting appropriately on the information is likely to result in benefits to them or to some cause important to them. This is, of course, neither a new nor particularly earth-shattering conclusion. What might be somewhat more revealing, however, are the conclusions emerging from COMP concerning *how* to generate confidence in the data that show the effectiveness of a general education program.

Focus on Specific Outcomes. The evaluation effort should focus on clearly specified knowledge and skills that students are expected to acquire as the result of a general education program, rather than on a set of common learning experiences. At least initially, the evaluation question should be: How well are students learning what is expected of them? The initial question should *not* be: What courses or types of courses should be required of all students? For probably very good reasons, administrators, faculty, students, and external audiences believe that descriptions of the learning activities cannot tell them much about the effectiveness of general education programs if they do not also have information about the learning outcomes. In most of the cases described above, there was little agreement among decision-makers as to what learning activities are effective or as to which work best precisely because there was little evidence at either the local institution or in the literature on higher education that would help them reach an agreement. Apparently, many approaches, including learning on one's own, may work well. It was found that people can agree, however, on whether or not the intended learning did or did not, in fact, take place. After the facts are established, an institution can begin to experiment with various ways of teaching and learning.

Focus on Important Outcomes. The evaluation effort should focus on the knowledge and skill areas that decision-makers will judge to be important. At least initially, the evaluation effort should focus on a core of generic knowledge and skills that are thought by the decision-makers to be important to functioning effectively in a wide variety of settings in our society. It is unrealistic to attempt to consider every area in which the general education program might have impact on students or every area in which student growth might take place. Little headway will be made in the evaluation process unless a core of important areas is tentatively identified for empirical study. It is only through such studies that the initial list of "important areas" can be verified or modified.

Among the cases cited above, there was a large variety in curricular design as well as in the goals and priorities set for the general education programs. In some cases, the objectives were vague. In others, the standards being applied varied considerably even within a single institution. In most of the cases, however, the decision-makers or the institutions could agree that there is a set of intended outcomes common to most general education programs.

The process by which each institution discovered what was important to its decision-makers varied from institution to institution: some institutions appointed special committees composed of representatives of relevant decision-makers; others used questionnaires, inventories, and surveys; several included literature surveys and exchange of ideas with other institutions and agencies. Most institutions used a combination of these approaches. COMP drew on the results of this process in order to create its list of the outcomes common to a great number of colleges and universities across the country.

Phrase Outcomes Clearly. The knowledge and skill areas identified as the focus of the evaluation should be described in terminology that all significant decision-makers can understand. The COMP list of outcomes, for example, reflects the effort not only to find a list of outcomes thought by decision-makers to be important but also to state those outcomes in language that can be understood easily by students, faculty, administrators, and various external publics.

Test the Ability to Apply Learnings. The assessment procedures used to measure student learning should go beyond measuring academic achievement to the evaluation of the student's ability to apply what has been learned to adult situations after graduation. Although it is not feasible to actually place students in such situations, COMP has shown that it is quite feasible to create simulation activities that require the application of knowledge and skills to problems and issues commonly confronted by adults. This extension of the evaluation process increases decision-makers' confidence in the information gained from an assessment of student learning. And the empirical evidence that COMP has obtained further supports this confidence: the evidence shows that test scores on simulation activities correlate highly with such indices of success as job supervisor ratings, the social or economic status of job function, participation in community volunteer activities, and the amount of continuing education pursued after the undergraduate program.

This type of learning assessment can also be enhanced by including a self-report inventory of the quality and quantity of participation in a variety of relevant activities outside of those required by courses in which students have enrolled. Such information would indicate the students' capabilities for functioning effectively in adult situations as well as their motivation for doing so.

Use Objective Techniques. Another COMP conclusion is that the techniques used to gather information about program effectiveness should be as objective as possible. This is critical if the goal is to produce data in which the decision-makers will have confidence. Since no one method of data collection is completely adequate, it is probably best to use two or three methods that will assess effectiveness from a number of perspectives, as Palola describes in Chapter Three. If the focus is on student learning, the expert judgment of faculty as well as opinion surveys and self-report inventories completed by students and alumni can be helpful. Feedback from community leaders and employers can also be useful. However, a more direct assessment of what students know and can do should also be attempted (by using standardized tests, for instance).

The testing format in which decision-makers are likely to have the most confidence is one that involves testing a group of entering freshmen and testing again those persons in the group who persist to graduation. Such comparison will give some indication of probable gains in student learning. In the interest of obtaining timely data, however, it is frequently appropriate first to test a representative sample of students near graduation in the spring of a review year and to follow that by testing a matched group of entering freshmen the following fall. Comparisons of the two groups will give some indication of probable gains in student learning.

In addition, confidence in the data will grow markedly among the decision-makers if the research format provides answers to a few more questions. How do senior scores compare to scores obtained by a sample of effectively functioning adults? How do the gains compare with people who have not engaged in a general education program? These question can only be answered if normative data is available for comparison. This is one of the chief advantages offered by a cooperative evaluation program such as COMP. In most of the cases described here, access to normative data from a nationally standardized instrument was critical to generating confidence in the data collected. The use of the assessment instrument itself, with its demonstrated validity and reliability, was also very important in instilling confidence in the information gathered.

Involve Decision-Makers Throughout. The evaluation should involve the decision-makers (or at least their representatives) in conceptualizing, planning, and implementing the data collection and in the analysis and dissemination of results. Again, Tom Hogan provides a participative model in Chapter Two. This means involving students, faculty, administrators, employers, and representatives from significant funding sources. Decision-makers are most likely to have confidence in data that they or their peers and colleagues have helped to collect and analyze. Decision-makers are also most likely to have confidence in data they understand. Peers and colleagues who have been involved in the data collection and analyses can be effective in communicating the results. This involvement is of critical importance.

Gaining the meaningful involvement of decision-makers in the evaluation process may not be an easy task. Students may not like taking tests. Faculty may be reluctant to take time from other interests to engage in a review. Administrators of general education programs may not be eager to have the programs evaluated. Persons external to the institution may not see why they should play a role in systematic program evaluation.

The institutions in COMP that have been successful in eliciting meaningful involvement have employed a number of strategies. No one strategy appears adequate to achieving the goal of involvement. Many institutions pay administrators, faculty, students and/or external decision-makers to participate in the evaluation process. This strategy is most frequently employed to induce students to take tests. Students will also respond favorably if the test is administered during class time or is offered in lieu of an academic requirement, such as a term paper or final examination. Some institutions make test participation by students a requirement in freshmen orientation or at graduation time. Many institutions provide nonmonetary reimbursement to students, faculty, administrators, alumni, employers, and so on for their participation; these "payments" include tickets to campus sporting or theatrical events, a dinner, or a ticket for a chance drawing for a stereo. Frequently, institutions will compensate faculty participants by reducing teaching or committee loads or by making participation a part of a faculty development plan.

It is important to have the decision-makers (or their representatives) involved in discussions about the need for evaluating educational programs. Such discussions, in turn, should stress the need for decision-makers to participate in the actual evaluation process. Once these needs are generally understood and agreed to by decision-makers, discussions can then turn to formulating a plan for evaluation. When there is general agreement on the plan, the chief administrative officer of the institution should tell all decision-makers about the importance of the evaluation effort and the plan to achieve the review. It is important to explain clearly how the results will be used, who has been involved in planning, who will be involved in the implementation of the plan, what the nature of their roles will be, how much time and effort will be required, what funding will be involved, and what time table will be followed. The initial communication should also specify the nature and extent of feedback of the results to the decision-makers.

The plan for evaluation should designate one person to manage the implementation phase. Following the initial announcement, this person should contact all those who will actually be involved in data collection, giving details of assessment activities, requesting written confirmation of willingness to cooperate, and specifying any cash payments or other compensation and inducements. Face-to-face contact with the director of the evaluation effort or with someone from the planning group who already knows the person being contacted is usually the most effective means of gaining cooperation. When this is too costly or impractical, telephone calls or letters can be used. Multiple contacts to each person are valuable, and follow-up contacts at various points in the evaluation process are helpful. If appropriate, those persons who will be taking examinations and/or completing inventories should be offered feedback on individual results as well as information about the program review.

Encourage Decision-Makers to Communicate the Need for Action. The benefits to be derived from acting appropriately on the data results should be communicated by the decision-maker participants in the evaluation effort to their counterparts. Presumably, the data results will lead to problems being corrected in the general education program, and they will document to all decision-makers that the program is worthy of support. Again, the most effective communicators of this message can be the decision-makers actually involved in the evaluation effort. Again, this involvement is so important that participants should be rewarded somehow for their work. Following data collection, the original group involved in planning the evaluation should meet to discuss plausible interpretations of the results. These discussions should serve as a background for the one person who will write a basic comprehensive report to be reviewed by the group.

The final report should represent a consensus of the interpretations, and possibly the recommendations, of the group. This report should be as candid and objective as possible. The interpretations and recommendations should be as flexible as possible in indicating possible directions for the future of the general education program. In order to help gain consensus on decisons about action to be implemented to improve the general education program, the report should present the widest range of plausible options. From this basic report, several reports should be generated; they will vary in format and length. Each additional report should be targeted to a specific group of decision-makers. Some reports will be brief brochures; others will be full pamphlets. These reports should be written in simple language and rely heavily on graphic presentations. They should specify in detail the implications of the data for the specific group of decision-makers for whom the report is designed. These various reports, together with oral communications from the decision-maker participants, should encourage other decision-makers to pay attention to the results of the evaluation study in making decisons relative to the general education program.

Summary

The effectiveness of general education programs can be measured, and the resulting information can lead to the improvement of the programs as well as help to maintain support for them. The amount of commitment to use the information in decision-making depends on the degree of confidence decision-makers have in the significance of the information itself and on the degree of confidence they have that acting appropriately on the information will result in benefits to them or to some cause important to them. The key to building confidence in decision-makers is involving them or their representatives in an evaluation effort that will measure objectively the areas of student learning that the decision-makers believe to be important.

Aubrey Forrest is director for instructional design and assessment at the American College Testing Program. He previously was director of assessment at Metropolitan State University. His Ph.D. in education is from Northwestern University.

*If institutional researchers really want to get their
studies used, they must become "change agents"—
skillful catalysts and facilitators of data-based
decisions and follow-through.*

The Institutional Researcher
as Change Agent

Stuart Terrass
Velma Pomrenke

Previous chapters remind us again and again that the traditional concep-
tion of the institutional researcher's role just won't do if we want to get
research used. Institutional researchers are not just data-gatherers and data
analysts, although the Association for Institutional Research (AIR) forums
consists of a frantic flow from computer processing to measurement and
statistics to modeling sessions. When two questions are asked of institutional research—is it useful, and is it used—the activity of simply manipu-
lating data makes a poor reply.

Certainly the job of institutional research is to "provide executive-
level management information appropriate to local decision-makers and
similar information to outside agencies" (Ridge, 1978, p. 1). "Provide
information," however, is far too mild a phrase for what is needed. Dressel's
definition is more dynamic: to carry out "studies which force administrators and faculty members to re-examine their goals as well as their practices" (Dressel, 1972, p. 310). He adds that institutional research's "ultimate
success depends less on the research findings than on the promotion of
action to alleviate functional weakness and to increase the effectiveness of
the institution" (pp. 49–50). What is implied is research that is accomplished and delivered so that it moves people to action, to change. That is

J. Lindquist (Ed.), *New Directions for Institutional Research: Increasing the
Utilization of Institutional Research*, no. 32. San Francisco: Jossey-Bass, December 1981.

73

the message of this book. And the message tells us that institutional researchers, like it or not, must become *change agents*—catalysts and facilitators of change in administrative and faculty practices. If they do not, they are likely to experience these familiar outcomes: studies that answer questions that were not asked; revised procedures that don't work because those they effect are not involved in the revision process; recommendations from outside consultants rejected primarily because they are made by "outsiders"; or a committee of knowledgeable and concerned individuals who meet for weeks but are never able to accomplish a task. In this chapter, we discuss the implications of the term, change agent, for the preparation and continuing professional development of institutional researchers.

The Change Process

It is obvious that none of us in higher education can escape change. Because of external forces (such as governmental controls and regulations, societal demands, and changing markets) and internal forces (such as the knowledge explosion, student and faculty demands, and fiscal restraints) colleges and universities exist in a highly dynamic, continually changing environment. To maintain viability, institutions in higher education must be responsive to the need for growth and change. Such growth and change can and should occur as the result of the careful planning of the next several decades. No matter how directly one sees institutional research functioning in this activity, it must include the role of a change agent.

We would expect little debate among institutional researchers about the responsibility for supporting the change process. It is hard to imagine an institutional researcher who views the educational environment or the major issues confronting it as anything but dynamic and changing. It would be equally difficult to expect someone in the profession to argue against the growing emphasis and need for planned change. However, it is *not* obvious that there is a general understanding of either the change process or of its potential ramifications for institutional research. Furthermore, although there is ample evidence that (either purposefully or intuitively) many in institutional research do function effectively as change agents, the authors find almost no recognition of this role in either the profession's literature or the forum topics. Hopefully, the following sections will help bridge that apparent gap.

Basic Change Notions. It is one thing to talk about the need for change but quite another thing to understand how change comes about. Although the literature on change is voluminous (Beckhard and Harris, 1977; Bennis, Benne, and Chin, 1969; Fessler, 1976; Lindquist, 1978; Lippitt, Watson, and Westley, 1958; and Tushman, 1974, are a few examples), a brief review of some basic concepts should serve as a foundation for discussing the role of change agent as applied to institutional research.

More than two decades ago, Lippitt, Watson, and Westley (1958) described change as a phase process. To effect change, a change agent must catalyze and facilitate (1) recognizing the need for change, (2) diagnosing the need for change, (3) examining alternative plans and choosing the preferred one, (4) implementing the plans, and (5) institutionalizing them. Others note that it is important to target the part of the organization that needs changing. Is change needed in the task of an organization, the technology whereby the task is accomplished, the people who implement the task, the structure that determines how the organization functions, or some combination (Leavitt, 1965)? Chin and Benne (1969) observe that change theories make very different assumptions regarding what it takes to change any aspect of one's organization. Some believe people are essentially rational, so the change agent's job is to garner the best available reason and evidence. Others feel that change is resisted primarily on the grounds of social attitudes and norms, so the change agent's main task is to ferret out those resistances and help reduce them. Others see change as a battle of competing interests; the change agent's principle responsibility is to get and use political power. Lindquist (1978) raises yet another possibility:

> Is it not possible to entertain the notion that humans are rational, social creatures who want to solve their hidden problems but also want to protect and enhance their vested interest? If we make such an assumption, we must combine our strategies for change (p. 9).

Institutional researchers too often deal as if their world were only rational: They must learn to function well at social, emotional, and political levels.

Research Use as Diffusion. Especially pertinent to research utilization is the literature on diffusion of innovations. Diffusion is the process by which information is communicated and used. Its purpose is nicely summarized by two of its leading scholars: (Rogers and Shoemaker, 1971, p. 1):

> The gap between what is known and what is effectively put to use needs to be closed. To bridge this gap, we must understand how new ideas spread from their source to potential receivers and understand the factors affecting the adoption of such innovations.

The knowledge base for diffusion has been both summarized and extended in the past decade by Havelock (1969) and Lindquist (1978, 1980). Their efforts have also been applied to the area of developing practical guides or manuals for the training of change agents (Havelock, 1972; Chickering and others, 1978). In a joint chapter, Havelock and

Lindquist (1980) define three distinct activities in the diffusion process: generation, dissemination, and utilization. They feel, however, that these activities (or processes) have been erroneously interpreted by others to be a neat, linear sequence in which these activities are unrelated to one another. Havelock and Lindquist believe that ideas will be more readily adopted or adapted if the innovation is strongly linked to the potential user's needs right from the beginning. Havelock proposes, therefore, a linkage model for planned change (1969, pp. 2–10). By linkage he means some kind of regularized pattern of communication between the knowledge development and use systems that will form a bond between them.

The eight stages or functions in the linkage model are: (1) calling attention to and articulating certain needs in a manner that will attract notice; (2) establishing a close interaction between the target audience and the developer of an innovation; (3) designing the relevant research and development activities in collaboration with the target audience; (4) solving the problems using the scientific method and looking to the practitioner for the identification of these problems; (5) translating research results into usable and practical terms for the practitioner; (6) planning carefully and allocating adequate resources to dissemination activities with major emphasis on audience/developer interaction; (7) assisting an adaptation process that will adjust an innovation to fit local concerns, structures, norms, and values; and (8) helping users create their own solutions largely out of their own resources in close interaction with the broader scientific and practitioner communities.

Lindquist's *adaptive development* model (1978) rests on Havelock's foundation but shifts the "knowledge producer" function, the essential problem-solver's role, from the external research and development expert to the practitioner. In this model, the principal change agent is the institutional leader; the institutional researcher becomes a consultant/facilitator to the problem solving accomplished by practitioners.

We believe these diffusion models can be particularly useful in considering the development, maintenance, or evaluation of linkages between institutional research and other departments or offices on campus. Earlier chapters offer practical examples of their usefulness. But who are the change agents who can combine their change assumptions with a complex diffusion process?

The Internal Change Agent. Planned change, from inception to fruition, can be an extremely complex process; many organizations, therefore, enlist the aid of an outsider, a professional change agent, to help plan, direct, and facilitate the process. Without detracting from the importance and need for these external change agents, we believe that organizations can and must develop a cadre of individuals within the organization with the necessary skills to become internal change agents. Only in this way will the organization be capable of rapid and appropriate response to the needs for change. Internal change agents are positive facilitators of change and of the change process who belong to the organization. Unlike the external change agent, whose change involvement and responsibilities are usually long term and comprehensive, the internal change agent's involvement will depend on the particular change situation and the responsibilities will depend on what he or she can contribute to a change team's effort. Planned change is not accomplished through the efforts of a single individual nor of a number of persons working independently; it can be successful only through cooperative teamwork. Thus, the role of internal change agents is to facilitate change while carrying out their normal organizational responsibilities, at the same time recognizing that this role is part of a team effort.

Any member of an organization can be a change agent—in an ideal situation all members would accept this role. Nevertheless, because of their position, some persons are more critical to the change process than others. We believe that a person in institutional research occupies one of those critical positions for institutions of higher education. As a major source of information for institutional management, this person will usually be involved in the initial stages of major change efforts begun at the executive level. At the same time, because most institutional research offices attempt to assist any other office requesting information or help, there is the potential for influencing change efforts on almost all levels of the institution.

Institutional researchers are naturally oriented to the team approach because of the nature of their field, the diversity of data and informational needs, of projects, and of areas of concern usually require both interoffice and intraoffice collaboration and teamwork. In addition, most institutional researchers are regularly members of ongoing or special committees, task forces, and the like. It would be difficult to find someone in the field who did not recognize the importance and necessity for teamwork. At the same time, the researcher's role is usually considered solitary. Learning to be a member or leader of a collaborative team will be a large part of the continuing development of the institutional researcher who works as a change agent.

In general, we see four areas of knowledge and skill especially important for internal change agents:

1. The change process and planned change theory, strategies, and so on
2. The nature and sources of resistance to change and how to deal with these
3. Interpersonal and intergroup relations
4. The whole area of leadership, management, and organizational development.

Because successful change agentry is a matter of attitude as well as skill (Wrightsman, 1977), we believe Fessler's list to be well worth tacking on one's office wall (Fessler, 1976, pp. 32–35). The change agent:

1. Accepts the fact that others have relevant experience and information and encourages them to share it with the group.
2. Constantly tries to broaden her knowledge, recognizing that a *technician who is first and foremost a technical expert is not suited to be an effective change agent* (emphasis is ours).
3. Works hard to enlarge the circle of people for whom she can feel genuine compassion.
4. Regards the ultimate objective as effecting a change, not gaining a popular following.
5. Helps people accept unpleasant situations that they cannot change and attempts to find elements in the situation that present new challenges.
6. Accepts his or her own limitations and helps others to do the same. At the same time, the change agent directs the attention of group members toward developing the talents they already have.
7. Keeps emotions and impulses under control and resists the temptation to expect preferential acceptance of his or her ideas.
8. Constantly tries to work for the common good even when that means giving up personal gratification; helps others to do the same.
9. Values other people's time as highly as his or her own and demonstrates this in the frugal use of others' time.

From Theory to Practice

How does an institutional researcher translate change theory into practice? A start is to begin to ask change questions when confronted with a possible study. What problem or issue is being raised by whom? For what purposes? What courses of action might flow from the inquiry? What possible difference can the inquiry make? What attitudes and values seem to underlie the request, and how will they get articulated in research use? What politics surround this issue and inquiry? Are those who will be affected properly involved in the study? Are its broader implications recognized? Essentially, these are questions not of the technical aspects of the inquiry but of its context—the factors influencing the use of its results.

Involve Your Audience Throughout. The second step is to plan ways to involve one's audience in all eight steps of the Havelock and Lindquist research utilization or diffusion model. A prior step, however, may be to convince one's superiors that institutional researchers themselves should be involved not just in Steps 3, 4, and 5—roughly the traditional role of developing and presenting studies—but also in needs assessment (Step 1), interactive dissemination (Step 6), adaptation of results to specific situations (Step 7), and integration of results into organizational problem solving (Step 8). In short, the institutional researcher as change agent will need sanction to become involved not only in research generation but in its dissemination and utilization phases.

We believe that, although neither time nor training will enable many institutional researchers to have the involvement suggested by this model, the institutional researcher can effectively perform as a change agent by following the spirit of the model. The first challenge would be to attempt to gain acceptance of the integration principle; thus, those directly involved on a continuous basis would work to achieve all eight steps that form the model. Secondly, by expressing a willingness to serve as a consultant or to provide feedback during the later stages of dissemination and utilization, the institutional researcher could be involved in later stages at a minimal level. To the degree that the model gains acceptance in other parts of the institution, the institutional researcher can aid in the development of other change agents. And to the degree that the institutional researcher can team with leaders of later phases, such as planners and professional development coordinators, the full research utilization process can be facilitated in an integrated manner.

Be a Team Facilitator. Most people in institutional research find that a considerable portion of their time is devoted to serving on committees, task forces, study teams, and the like. It is here that they may shine as change agents or, equally important, serve as role models for other prospective change agents. Usually, the impetus for including the institutional researcher as a member of such groups does not include a recognition of their role as a change agent; nevertheless, we believe that this may become a very important role as institutions move toward planned change activities with an increased need for internal change agents. When the institutional researcher functions as a member of a group, he or she must attempt to have the group recognize and consider appropriate strategies and tactics for change as well as a broader understanding of the change process itself. To this end the institutional researcher must develop satisfactory and successful interpersonal and intergroup relations. Teamwork, networks, and linkages that will promote and support an effective change process must be strengthened.

The institutional researcher must recognize two things: (1) he or she has a responsibility to contribute as a change agent no matter how the other group members perceive and function in their roles, and (2) the larger the number of persons that can be guided or convinced to be change agents, the greater the chance that institutional and individual needs will be met. Again, developing more effective interpersonal and intergroup relations involves risk. Because groups generally include both peers and superiors, moving beyond the single role of information source may be perceived as threatening. It is important, therefore, for the institutional researcher to develop the best possible "people skills" such as listening, communication, perception, feedback, group roles, team building, problem solving, conflict management, and so on. Without these skills, the role of change agent is practically impossible to fulfill.

What we have suggested thus far is that, in addition to the traditional roles for institutional researchers, there is the concomitant role of change agent. This function—the positive facilitation of the change process—can take place whether one is serving as an information source for decision-makers, a more traditional researcher, or as a committee or group member. It seems obvious that the several roles are interdependent; in like manner, each seems to help support the others, the requisite knowledge and skills for one being applicable to all the others. However, this is not to say that effective performance in one role guarantees or implies effective performance in the others. The skills and knowledge for any one role are not sufficient for each of the others.

If one recognizes the multiple roles of institutional research, develops the knowledge base and skills for each, and applies these, we believe that the institutional researcher's potential service to the institution will expand geometrically, if not exponentially. At the same time, the individual's sense of accomplishment may well experience a corresponding increase.

A Change Agent Development Program

One final set of questions remains to be answered: Is it possible and practical to develop internal change agents? If so, how might it be done? And, more specifically, how might one train those in institutional research to become change agents?

Some years ago the present leadership at the University of Akron recognized the need for a change in leadership style that would be more responsive to the needs of a complex organization in a dynamic, shifting environment. Supported by the W. K. Kellogg Foundation as part of a larger "network of change," the University of Akron's team leadership development program sought to promote a participative and collaborative mode of dealing with the changes thrust upon higher education by the shifting dynamics of our society (W. K. Kellogg Foundation, 1978). An obvious aim of the program was the development of a pool of internal change agents. A heterogeneous mix, both horizontally (across disciplines) and vertically (by status), of faculty and administrators participated in each of the four "classes" (twenty-five to thirty persons per class) that completed the program. Each class included a three-day retreat and eight weekly one-day sessions. The initial emphasis was on developing interpersonal, intragroup, and intergroup communications; later, the emphasis shifted to understanding the structure and dynamics of university organization and operation; and finally, the emphasis was shifted to issues in higher education and specific problems and needs of the University of Akron as an urban institution. After completing the sessions, participants in each class were given the opportunity to convert learning into actual practice through task forces and internships.

The success and acceptance of the program on the part of the participants was particularly evident from the large number of short-term team leadership workshops and seminars that were requested and held within work units of the university. University acceptance was demonstrated by the establishment of the Office of Team Leadership Development as well as the submission of a proposal to extend the concept to students at the university and to community leaders, as well as to faculty and administrators. This university/community program, also funded by the Kellogg Foundation, is still in progress and has stimulated many shorter-term programs in the community as well as on campus. Since 1976, some 1,500 persons at the university and in the community have been involved in the program in some way.

A Workshop on the Institutional Researcher as Change Agent

In the process of working together on team leadership efforts on the Akron campus, we frequently discussed the applicability of concepts of the team leadership program to institutional research, particularly the concept of the change agent role. The AIR forum held in Atlanta in May, 1980, provided an opportunity to extend these concepts into the arena of institutional research. Our proposal for a workshop called "The Institutional Researcher as a Change Agent" was accepted and the workshop was conducted with approximately forty participants. The workshop was based on the assumption that there are two major ingredients in all human interaction—content and process. Attention and training, particularly for technical specialists such as institutional researchers, is usually directed toward the first ingredient, the subject or content. The second—what happens between and to persons as they pursue their tasks—is often overlooked even though we know that "people problems" and their solutions often determine the success or failure of a task. Very few programs at earlier forums had addressed this issue and fewer still had provided the opportunity to practice the skills needed to close the gap between knowledge and application. The objectives of the workshop, therefore, were to enable participants to examine and practice the skills essential to the role of change agent through an experiential format. Because the workshop can be conducted on an individual campus with slight modification, we offer the design here.

The specific goals for the two-part six-hour workshop were:

1. To increase participants' skills in serving as internal change agents and/or consultants within their organization.
2. To help participants increase their skills in communicating and disseminating institutional research data.
3. To facilitate the sharing of experiences concerning institutional research among participants, with particular emphasis on process experiences.

The workshop was designed around four learning modules. The modules and their purposes were as follows: (1) "Dynamics of Change": to present change strategies more apt to ensure that institutional research data will be used in the acceptance and implementation of change; (2) "Perception and Values": to demonstrate how the dynamics of perception can help or hinder the acceptance of institutional researchers and their data, as well as to become aware of personal and organizational values that impact change strategies; (3) "Group Dynamics": to heighten awareness of group dynamics (roles, norms, communication channels, effects of status) in order to understand these dynamics when they are encountered by the institutional researcher; and (4) "Integration of Process Concepts": to provide an experience in which participants can integrate the various concepts into a simulated change situation.

Each learning module was designed around an experiential and interactive component in which the participants were given the opportunity to experience a process concept directly related to their professional needs and interests. For example, in order to make it possible for participants to learn from one another, they were divided into small groups in which they introduced themselves, described their positions, and identified change issues from their vantage point in institutional research.

For the "Perceptions and Values" module, participants were divided into a simulated task force and assigned roles such as vice-president for academic affairs, director of admissions and records, a senior undergraduate student, a member of the Board of Trustees, and, of course, the director of institutional research. The task was as follows:

Table University's president, concerned about growing costs and the likelihood of stable or falling enrollments, has appointed a task force with the following charge: In order to ensure this institution's fiscal stability and to more equitably distribute the cost of education to our student-body, it has been suggested that this institution change its fee structure such that course fees would more adequately reflect the relative cost for each course—by program and level—within the framework of the full university course offerings. Your task force is to determine whether or not this is a viable action, how it could be accomplished, and recommend a plan for accomplishing this goal.

In the course of the conversation, participants became more aware that people in differing roles and positions in an organization will approach suggested changes from differing viewpoints. A successful change agent is aware of those potential differences and tries to facilitate the mediation of those differences. This experiential and interactive approach serves several purposes: it facilitates professional sharing; it helps participants to explore professional issues in greater depth and to generate alternative solutions to common problems; and it provides an opportunity to experiment with a new mode of behavior within a relatively safe environment. It is an approach that facilitates transference of learning—that is, learning and the application of that learning are linked together in a way that encourages back-home application.

Were the purposes of the workshop achieved? It would be foolish to suggest it was an unqualified success, given the brief time (six hours) and the ambitious nature of the goals. Nevertheless, anonymous evaluation comments lead us to believe it had a positive effect. Some of the comments were:

> This workshop activated me in analyzing my own behavior, giving tools to achieve better results in groups. I think I will work with my people (groups) with new, other views.
>
> Most valuable ideas—the de-emphasis of "data, things, etc." and the emphasis on "people." As a group we have the stereotype of working like mice in cubicles with our figures and our papers and we need, horribly, to develop our "human" traits and skills.
>
> Helped me to see myself and AIR as more than data-gathering, report-generating arm of the chancellor.
>
> I believe that we are certainly going to be in the limelight for serving the institutions because the hour of need is here now, and using people skills will help us to do a more efficient job.
>
> I think the concept of change agent is serving to wake up some of the members AIR. I hear a great deal of moaning about "poor me," unlistened to, unappreciated, etc. The workshop should make them aware of the need to take a pro-active stance.

On the basis of these evaluations, it would appear to be useful to provide further training in "people skills" for institutional researchers.

Summary

Throughout this paper, we have attempted to view the role of institutional research from a different perspective. Although the change agent role—frequently identified by different terminology—may be an accepted function for the institutional researcher by the profession, the knowledge and skills required to be a change agent command scant attention in either the literature or the AIR forum programming. An alteration of this situation seems long overdue and particularly critical to the profession in light of the increasing and changing expectations for institutional research.

The knowledge, skills, and attitudes of a change agent are not necessarily inherent in the technical competencies of the institutional researcher; therefore, continuing education in technical areas will not ensure a similar advance in change agent capabilities. In addition, although individual initiative may lead one to improve change agent skills, professional neglect of the topic is hardly conducive to fostering such initiative. Even if one assumes that all institutional researchers already possess the necessary change agent knowledge and skills, it is unrealistic to assume that there is nothing new to be learned in this area. Just as technical competencies must be updated, interpersonal and intergroup skills and change competencies require re-examination and revision.

In closing, we would like to make three recommendations for consideration by institutional researchers, individually and as a profession. We believe that acceptance and implementation of these proposals will significantly improve the capability of institutional research to meet the challenges of the profession and will at the same time increase the utility and service of institutional research to individual institutions.

1. Greater attention must be given to people skills and change process skills in institutional research literature and AIR forum programming.

2. Training programs, nationally and locally, should be developed and implemented to teach or update change agent skills.

3. Institutional researchers should make greater use of the wealth of knowledge and applications in related fields (such as organizational development, diffusion of innovations, communication, small group theory) to improve and expand their usefulness to their institutions.

References

Beckhard, R. and Harris, R. T. *Organizational Transitions: Managing Complex Change.* Reading, Mass.: Addison-Wesley, 1977.

Bennis, W. G.,Benne, K.D., and Chin, R. (Eds.). *The Planning of Change.* (2nd ed.) New York: Holt, Rinehart and Winston, 1969.

Chickering, A., and others. *Developing the College Curriculum.* Washington, D.C.: Council for the Advancement of Small Colleges, 1978.

Chin, R., and Benne, K. D. "General Strategies for Effecting Changes in Human Systems." In Bennis, W. G., Benne, K. D., and Chin, R. (Eds.), *The Planning of Change.* (2nd ed.) New York: Holt, Rinehart and Winston, 1969.

Dressel, P. L. and Associates. *Institutional Research in the University: A Handbook.* San Francisco: Jossey-Bass, 1972.

Fessler, D. R. *Facilitating Community Change: A Basic Guide.* La Jolla, Calif.: University Associates, 1976.

Havelock, R. G. *Planning for Innovation Through the Utilization of Scientific Knowledge.* Ann Arbor, Mich.: Institute for Social Research, 1969.

Havelock, R. G. *Training for Change Agents: A Guide to the Design of Training Programs in Education and Other Fields.* Ann Arbor, Mich.: Institute for Social Research, 1972.

Havelock, R., and Lindquist, J. "A Conceptual Framework for Increasing the Impact." In J. Lindquist (Ed.), *Increasing the Impact.* Battle Creek: W. K. Kellogg Foundation, 1980.

Leavitt, H. "Applied Organizational Change in Industry." In J. March (Ed.), *Handbook of Organizations.* Chicago: Rand McNally, 1965.

Lindquist, J. *Strategies for Change.* Washington, D.C.: Council for the Advancement of Small Colleges, 1978.

Lindquist, J. (Ed.). *Increasing the Impact.* Battle Creek, Mich.: W. K. Kellogg Foundation, 1980.

Lippitt, R., Watson, J., and Westley, B. *The Dynamics of Planned Change: A Comparative Study of Principles and Techniques.* New York: Harcourt Brace, 1958.

Ridge, J. W. "Organizing for Institutional Research." In Perry, R. R. (Ed.). *AIR Professional File.* Tallahassee, Fla.: Association for Institutional Research, fall, 1978.

Rogers, E. M., and Shoemaker, F. F. *Communication of Innovation.* New York: Free Press, 1971.

Tushman, M. *Organizational Change: An Exploratory Study and Case History.* ILR Paperback No. 15. Ithaca: New York State School of Industrial and Labor Relations, Cornell University, 1974.

University of Akron, W. K. Kellogg Foundation. *Program for the Development of Team Leadership at an Urban University, Final Report: January 1976–February 1978.* Akron, Ohio: University of Akron, 1978.

Wrightsman, L. S. *Social Psychology.* (2nd ed.) Monterey, Calif.: Brooks/Cole, 1977.

Stuart Terrass is coordinator of the Office of Institutional Studies and Research at the University of Akron in Ohio. An institutional researcher for the past thirteen years, he has also served as registrar and in student personnel administration. For a year he had part-time responsibilities as a trainer in the team leadership development program. Mr. Terrass holds a master's degree in history.

Velma Pomrenke is coordinator of the Office of Team Leadership Development at the University of Akron in Ohio. She has planned, coordinated, and taught many training events for such diverse groups as university faculty, administrators, staff, and students as well as community, state, and national groups representing social service, education, business, and professional organizations. Dr. Pomrenke holds a master's degree in education and a Ph.D. in social psychology.

*This concluding chapter summarizes the volume's
main points, suggests additional techniques for quick
but useful action research, and offers basic references
for the professional development of institutional
research use.*

Quick, Dirty, and Useful

Jack Lindquist

Institutional researchers are all too accustomed to the "quick and dirty"
computer run on matters of daily administrative trauma such as cash flow
and enrollment count. Dropping everything to do such studies is a nui-
sance, but at least the data get used. Administrators know they need those
figures to judge financial well-being, and they usually initiate the request.
The evidence may not have the solidity and elegance of a full-blown
financial analysis, but it is far better than guesswork.

Institutional research on academic well-being rarely has such a
short time-line or eager audience. The slow survey, about no one is sure
quite what, done for no one can remember just whom, is the more typical
assignment. This prompts a lot of work, with sometimes fascinating and
important results but with little payoff. Contributors to this volume discuss stronger approaches, more closely entwined with academic decision
making, but most of these modes cannot match the immediate usefulness of
those quick and dirty enrollment counts.

There are, however, analogs to such studies. They are not, for the
most part, familiar tools in the traditional institutional research kit. They
are not easy. They are rarely done. They are, however, potentially powerful
ways to obtain quick, useful, systematic insights into academic health. And
their action follow-up is built into the design. This chapter outlines several
such "quick, dirty, but useful" strategies for getting data, and getting the
data used, to improve academic practices. The chapter also discusses the

J. Lindquist (Ed.), *New Directions for Institutional Research: Increasing the
Utilization of Institutional Research*, no. 32. San Francisco: Jossey-Bass, December 1981.

87

skills institutional researchers need to develop, or recruit, in order to meet the very considerable demands placed on those who lead such inquiries. But before getting to these details, let us summarize the lessons of previous chapters.

Involve, Involve

Hogan, Palola, Forrest, and Pomrenke and Terrass—each finds that uninvolving research is unused research. A researcher's audience needs to feel that these are *our* questions on issues of concern to *us,* answered in ways *we* understand and trust, with implications *we* buy. The best way to generate that feeling is to do institutional research not for but with one's audience. It is a more time-consuming, messy process than studies conducted in isolation. It constantly is on the rim of respectability among traditional researchers. It takes facilitating skills that are often not part of a researcher's preparation or interest. But without audience involvement, institutional research can become a stack of printouts signifying nothing.

Be Systematic but Flexible

Hogan, Palola, and Forrest have elaborate evaluation systems. Each system is technically sophisticated. Action research is not loosey-goosey. But each author stresses flexibility, the willingness and ability to adjust one's design and redefine one's technique to fit the concerns and learning styles of one's audience. The researcher who has "the only way to do it" has loneliness.

Learn to Be a Change Agent

Terrass and Pomrenke address the point directly, but each previous contributor also emphasizes the "change agent" skills necessary if researchers are to get their valuable information used. Those skills include the ability to write various kinds of reports for various audiences, as Palola notes. They include the involving skills that Hogan's project so nicely exemplify. "Catalyst," "facilitator," and "team" are repeated words in Terrass and Pomrenke's chapter, each dramatizing the interpersonal dimension of research use. To become good both with data and with people is a large agenda in professional development for institutional researchers, but the experiences of these contributors reveal the power of both such skills.

Vary and Compare

Palola especially advises us to vary our research perspectives, while Forrest demonstrates the power of local comparisons with national norms.

Each is saying that a person needs contrast in order to judge the validity of evidence. The audience needs to know the answers to questions such as: Do others, by different means, see the same thing? Are our results up to results in other, credible colleges? "Researcher One-Note" will not capture the conviction of many.

These are but four of the general lessons emerging from prior pages. Each chapter offers further suggestions in great detail. Such conclusions, entirely confirming the action-research framework outlined in Chapter One, lie at the base of the following quick, dirty, but useful tactics for research use.

A Week in the Life of . . .

One important question of academic well-being is, "What is going on out there?" What do diverse students and faculty do all day? What do they think about? What influence, on a daily basis, does our curriculum have on them? Such questions invite long, careful study, and they deserve it. But they can also be viewed in snapshots, which, systematically taken, can be much less distorted than the anecdotal evidence on which we usually rely.

One such snapshot would be a narrative "week in the life of" a sample of students, faculty, and/or administration. Robert Blackburn and associates' brief but vivid protrait of the University of Michigan's "Pilot Program" comes to mind (Blackburn, 1968). In such studies, the members of the sample are asked to keep a daily log, with hourly entries, on what they did, said, and read (in the left column) and what they were thinking at the time (in the right). A social science or journalism class desiring some interview practice can be recruited to sit down with the participants twice in the week to go over the logs and flesh out the entries. When the week is over, analyze the content of the logs for common themes and issues and the ways learning, teaching, or administrating seem to be enhanced or blocked. Then get participants and relevant academic decision-makers together to read and hear the "story," rather the "stories," of that week. This kind of data should be presented with specific actions and thoughts well in view, rather than in summary form, for the latter loses the sharpness of these lives in progress. The institutional researcher as storyteller becomes the role here, and those who were trained as social scientists would do well to invite an English or theater professor to lend a hand.

An Incident in the Life of . . .

A variation on this snapshot is swooping in on a single incident, sometimes called "critical" (but it may be just average), in the lives of students, faculty, or administration. The assignment often is, "Pick a specific event that seemed important for you as a student, teacher, and administrator or which seemed to capture an effective (average, ineffective) moment in your work. Describe it in detail—what happened first, second, and so on, who said what, and describe what you were thinking and feeling at the time."

Ask enough folks until you begin to discover patterns or themes emerging from the average, important, effective moments in the lives of students, professors or administrators. Then share these incidents, plus the themes, with study participants and relevant others. Ask that hard question, "So what?" What do these patterns tell us about what is needed, in the person and the situation, to create a productive learning, teaching, or administrative experience around here? Now, how do we go about it?

Argyris and Schon (1974) use this as the primary data-gathering device in their executive training. Here, though, they use it to contrast a leader's (could be a teacher's or student's) theory of action (how I should and hopefully do act) and theory in use (how I actually act and the theory of leadership that my actions imply). I have found the device powerful in faculty and administrative development. This use blurs, quite appropriately, the roles of institutional researcher and faculty/administrative "developer." Both researcher and developer must gather and use data to aid improvement of institutional practices. Often, the marriage of the former's research skills and the latter's people skills forms a powerful research utilization team.

Participant Interviews and Analyses

Another version of divergent data gathering and feedback is to ask a study's participants to be its data-gatherers and analysts by interviewing one another, or by listening to taped interviews, and then analyzing them together. Both techniques tend to be especially handy at workshops in which key institutional leaders are brought together to inquire into academic effectiveness. Interview questions might concern the other person's hopes, past high or low points, current enjoyments and frustrations, and learnings from all this personal experience regarding the institution's academic effectiveness. Particularly powerful are men's interviews of women (and vice versa), whites of blacks, faculty of students or administrators, nonhandicapped of handicapped, young students of older. Robert Barry of Loyola University has a nice design in which a current student interviews a faculty member about what it was like to be a student "back then"; then the faculty member gets a picture of student experience now. Jack Noonan of Virginia Commonwealth University conducts an open-ended interview of college teachers and produces audio tapes of actual classes; these tapes are used to kick off faculty discussions of college teaching. In this instance, one's audience members become not the data-gatherers but the analysts. A variation of this technique, using "video vignettes" of teaching to stimulate discussion, has been developed by Robert Menges (1980) of Northwestern University.

Whether one invites audience members to be data gatherers or analysts, the idea is the same: researcher, get out of the way! Put your audience into direct contact with the data so that their listening, seeing, and analyzing can be done free of a midwife. Not that the researcher becomes extraneous! The job of helping one's audience tease insights out of these interviews and out of their own experiences is complex work, without which discussion can be of little use to anyone.

Learning by Doing

Experiential learning is the primary way students learn to learn, faculty to teach, and administrators to administrate. They observe it and do it. They learn through trial and error, through practice. Few go through formal training for, or read up on, these roles. It stands to reason that if a researcher hopes to enable faculty or administrators to gain new perspectives on their craft, they are likely to need fresh experiences, not just data about someone else's experiences. This need becomes especially apparent when one considers that most academicians have seen and used only one approach to education, the one that is a subject-centered course taught by lecture, discussion, paper, and exam, conducted in "classes" of 5 to 500, reliant on print and professor as principal learning resources, and graded on the normal curve. God gave this formula to Moses, written on the backs of the tablets, and it is higher learning. How are professors to get interested in the many promising alternatives of the 1980s if this sacred model is the only one they have experienced?

How can we do institutional research as experiential learning? Field trips, role playing, simulation, participant observation: these are the researcher's tools for this kind of quick, dirty, but useful inquiry. Take a target group to an innovative institution or department to see how it works and to talk to the participants. In a workshop setting, ask faculty to play a student role in a classroom or advising session. Ask an administrator to do an "in-basket" exercise in administrative problem solving. A whole governance situation might be experienced in a role-playing simulation so that people feel what it is like to be a student or dean. These experiences may be of familiar practices, aimed at gaining new insight into them, or of innovative practices, aimed at broadening one's perspective on how academic work can be done.

Researchers who use experiential inquiry will need to be good at it or to find faculty who use this method in their teaching. Careful orientation to the experience, skillful facilitation of it, and thoughtful debriefing are, again, not traditional institutional research skills, but they are critical to the success of this mode. An ironic problem in leading such activities is that, despite experiential learning's being the *informal* way students, faculty, and administration learn to do their work, they are unused to this approach in *formal* learning situations, especially as serious research. It helps to provide them with brief data and theory presentations—with the full story in handouts—so that one's audience feels there is solid academic substance to the proceedings. Facilitator grace in easing folks into active learning will be no small contribution to the inquiry.

Group Diagnosis

A device proved useful in several colleges when a quick diagnosis of educational problems is needed is a series of one-hour "group diagnosis" sessions with various campus groups. The design, like the earlier ones, is not nearly so complex as the facilitating and synthesizing skill needed to pull it off.

An hour is set aside with groups of fifteen or so from department faculties, administrative offices, or student classes. Three questions are raised. What strengths do you see in this program—the things we must preserve? What weaknesses or problems do you see—the things needing immediate attention? How might these problems be resolved? During the brainstorming session, every response to these questions is written on newsprint. After a spurt of perceptions are listed, the leader attempts a quick summary so that many items are reduced to four or five key categories under general strengths, problems, or improvement strategies. Checking the categories with the group helps confirm, in audience minds, their accuracy and validity (for instance, we all seem to think we have a tremendously diverse student-body, which our traditional curriculum and teaching is missing more than it hits). Then the group is asked to brainstorm ways to start solving the listed problems. From this list, a summary of "next steps" is created on the spot.

At this point, audience members may be asked to volunteer for special task forces to work on the problems, or this input may be directed to appropriate governance groups. If the second and more common tactic is used, plan to go through the group interview with this appropriate committee or office so its members also "own" the results. Input usually disappears into some hole to China precisely because it is not the decision-makers' insight but someone else's.

Student Ratings as Formative Feedback

Institutional researchers are often stuck with the computer analyses of student instructional ratings, but rarely do they have much of a role in getting this information used. Because most ratings occur at the end of a course, too late to improve that particular teaching/learning experience or to ask participants to amplify their responses, they end up used mainly in personnel judgments, not in academic improvement.

Faculty development leaders such as Glenn and Bette Erickson at the University of Rhode Island again show institutional researchers an alternative. Have students rate the teaching of faculty volunteers *during* a course. Perhaps supplement these numbers with interviews and observations. Then sit down with the faculty member, possibly with a student "helping panel" from the class, to discuss the results and to identify what needs to be preserved and what needs to be improved. The same process can be used with a department or program rather than one class as the focus. The method, as developed at the University of Massachusetts, is described in detail, replete with instruments, in Bergquist and Phillips (1978).

Facilitating Collaborative Inquiry

All these quick but useful data-gathering and feedback techniques as well as the methods of earlier chapters do use systematic inquiry, the institutional researcher's stock in trade. But the methods are nontraditional. The audience and the subjects of inquiry become active participants. The researcher becomes not just the data expert but the facilitator of others' inquiry, as Tom Hogan explains in Chapter Two and as the action-research model in Chapter One outlines. Terrass and Pomrenke, in Chapter Five, discuss many of the people skills needed to play this kind of change agent role. In other publications, I detail some of the tactics and skills needed for this role (Chickering and others, 1978; Lindquist and Clark, 1979). Let me summarize here this volume's constant emphasis on the institutional researcher as facilitator of collaborative inquiry.

One of the first things to learn is the level of one's own facilitative skills: listening, giving oral "feedback," managing group process and conflict, assessing and responding to personal and interpersonal needs. Informally, ask a trusted and candid colleague to share insights into how well you facilitate group process and problem solving. More formally, sign up for campus or off-campus training workshops in basic human interaction, then group facilitation. Prepare to work at this development throughout your career. After twenty years of training and practice, I still find myself short on the skill needed to untangle certain interpersonal problems that stand in the way of effective research use.

A second development agenda item should be the design and management of collaborative inquiry, "action research." Again, local colleagues who use group studies and experiential learning in their teaching can lend peer assistance. Local professors who use group interview, critical incident, and case methods of data gathering and analysis are other helpful resources. Formal training programs in data-based organizational and professional development can deepen that knowledge and skill.

A third professional development area would be information diffusion and networking. One should learn how to attend to such diffusion factors as relative advantages, complexity, compatibility, adaptability, observability, and trialability in sharing data or innovative answers to problems raised in diagnoses. One should learn how to assess one's social and political system of communication so information can spread from the eager few to the more cautious and skeptical many through "opinion leaders" and "gatekeepers." One should learn how to build and maintain support groups and influence networks. Local experts in communication of innovations and political systems can be of help, as can formal training in innovation diffusion.

Part of effective information linkage is a fourth area for institutional researcher development—learning about alternative administrative and faculty practices. A clear need to change is not enough; you also need a promising solution. Often, knowledge of that new alternative helps clarify a problem, as when a professor does not get worked up about teaching to the average until he discovers individualized education, which tells him teaching to only one segment of a class is not only ineffective but unnecessary. So, the institutional researcher who wants to facilitate collaborative inquiry will need to keep well up on new alternatives in college administration and teaching. Here, nearby higher education centers, the *Chronicle of Higher Education,* this *New Directions* series, and other current publications help, as do the many workshops and conferences on new trends in higher learning. A staff seminar on such matters could go far toward making institutional researchers ready resources for that critical question following diagnosis, "Now what?"

A word of caution. There are dozens of handbooks and workshops on interpersonal process, collaborative inquiry, innovation diffusion, networking. Most, however, are ignorant of the collegiate context and conducted in a manner that rubs academicians the wrong way. Seek those that show sensitivity to the peculiarities of college and university systems, to facilitating the inquiry of professors and deans, to how innovations flow and networks operate in postsecondary education.

The references listed below, integrated into a regular staff development program for institutional research use, should get you off to a good start. With limited outside consultation and by using portions of regular staff meetings plus semi-annual retreats as development time, such a program can be developed at low cost. The payoff in actually getting institutional research used is well worth this limited investment.

References

Here are a few practical references which are sensitive to the collegiate context:

Argyris, C., and Schön, D. *Theory in Practice: Increasing Professional Effectiveness.* San Francisco: Jossey-Bass, 1974.

Bergquist, W., and Phillips, S. *Handbook for Faculty Development.* Vols. 1 and 2. Washington, D.C.: Council for the Advancement of Small Colleges, 1975 and 1978.

Although aimed at persons in faculty development, these volumes include many research instruments and action-research techniques that are highly useful to institutional researchers.

Blackburn, R., and associates. "The Pilot Program." In *Memo to Faculty.* Ann Arbor: Center for Research on Learning and Teaching, 1968.

Chickering, A., Halliburton, D., Bergquist, W., and Lindquist, J. *Developing the College Curriculum.* Washington, D.C.: Council for the Advancement of Small Colleges, 1978.

This volume includes discussion of the educational issues, practical examples, and action-research process a campus team can use to obtain serious re-examination of local curricular and teaching practices.

Lindquist, J. *Increasing the Impact of Social Innovations.* Battle Creek, Mich.: W. K. Kellogg Foundation, 1980.

Information-diffusion theory and practice are synthesized here, including several case examples in the collegiate context plus practical tips on sharing information through reports, workshops, technical assistance, and other means.

Lindquist, J., and Clark, T. *Sourcebook.* Memphis, Tenn.: Institute for the Advancement of Small Colleges, 1978.

Here are detailed case histories of action-research efforts in six small colleges and two universities, augmented by synthesis of research on planned change and collegiate organization. The book's concluding framework, "adaptive development," underlies the strategy described in this *New Directions* sourcebook.

Lindquist, J., and Clark, T. *Sourcebook.* Memphis, Tenn.: Institute for Academic Improvement, Memphis State University, 1979.

Sikes, W., Schlesinger, L., and Seashore, C. *Renewing Higher Education from Within.* San Francisco: Jossey-Bass, 1974.

This slim volume reports team efforts to improve colleges through action research and offers many tips on that strategy.

Jack Lindquist is president at Goddard College. Previously he served as director of the Institute for Academic Improvement at Memphis State University, the Kellogg Use of Innovations Project at the University of Michigan, and the Strategies for Change and Knowledge Utilization Project of the Union for Experimenting Colleges and Universities. His Ph.D. in higher education is from the University of Michigan.

Index

A

Action research: analysis of, 3-25; beginning steps in, 33-35, 36; characteristis of, 40-43; client ownership of, 5, 88; and climate for change, 12-13; components of, 7-24; concept of, 3-4; concluding evaluation in, 38-39; context for, 30-31; and contract assistance, 55-56; cooperation and independence in, 39-40; critical incident for, 89-90; and cultural norms, 6-7; and data feedback, 17-18; and data validation, 18-21; example of, 27-43; experiential learning for, 91-92; flexibility in, 88; follow-up structures for, 55; group diagnosis for, 92; and implementation of innovation, 13-17; meetings for, 35, 37; multiple perspectives and channels in, 45-58; and need for change, 9-12; participant interviews and analysis for, 90-91; participants in, 31-33; and problem solving, 4-6; process of, 37-38; purpose and design in, 17-18; quick techniques for, 87-96; and solution assessment, 12; and student ratings, 92-93; tenets and strategies of, 4-6; triangulation of measures in, 9, 43-58; vary and compare in, 88-89; week's log for, 89
Akron, University of, 80-81, 85
Alkin, M. C., 28, 43
American College Testing Program (ACT), 60, 61
Argyris, C., 7, 25, 90, 95
Association for Institutional Research (AIR), 73, 81-83, 84
Attrition, feedback on, 57

B

Barry, R., 90
Beckhard, R., 74, 84

Bell, C., Jr., 4, 25
Benne, K. D., 74, 75, 84
Bennis, W. G., 74, 84
Bergquist, W., 25, 93, 95
Blackburn, R., 89, 95
Bloom, B. S., 42, 43
Bradley, A. P., Jr., 51, 58
Braskamp, L. A., 28, 43
Brown, R. D., 28, 43
Buhl, L. C., 2, 3-25, 27, 41, 45, 52

C

Carlson, D., 29, 43
Carnegie Foundation for the Advancement of Teaching, 59
Cattell, J. M., 28
Change: assessing need for, 9-12; climate supporting, 12-13; concepts of, 74-75; diffusion of, 75-76; implementation of, 13-17; and improving implementation, 15-17; involvement in, 78-79; practice of, 78-80; process of, 74-78
Change agents: analysis of, 73-85; characteristics of, 77-78, 88; development program for, 80-81; as facilitators, 79-80; internal, 76-78; workshop for, 81-83
Chickering, A., 13, 25, 75, 84, 93, 95
Chin, R., 74, 75, 84
College Outcome Measures Project (COMP): analysis of, 60-71; for assessing innovation, 61-62; cases using, 61-65; and clear phrasing, 67; and communicating need for action, 70-71; confidence in, 65-71; and external degrees, 62; and external judges, 62-63; and important outcomes, 66-67; and internal judges, 63-65; and involvement of decision-makers, 68-70; objective techniques in, 68; outcomes identified in, 60-61; and specific outcomes, 66; and tests of application of learning, 67-68
Confidentiality, protection of, 53
Costs, learning, evaluation of, 46-47

STATEMENT OF OWNERSHIP, MANAGEMENT, AND CIRCULATION
(Required by 39 U.S.C. 3685)

1. Title of Publication: New Directions for Institutional Research. A. Publication number: USPS 098-830. 2. Date of filing: September 30, 1981. 3. Frequency of issue: quarterly. A. Number of issues published annually: four. B. Annual subscription price: $30 institutions; $18 individuals. 4. Location of known office of publication: 433 California Street, San Francisco (San Francisco County), California 94104. 5. Location of the headquarters or general business offices of the publishers: 433 California Street, San Francisco (San Francisco County), California 94104. 6. Names and addresses of publisher, editor, and managing editor: publisher—Jossey-Bass Inc., Publishers, 433 California Street, San Francisco, California 94104; editor—Marvin Peterson, Center for Study of Higher Education, University of Michigan, Ann Arbor, MI 48109; managing editor—JB Lon Hefferlin, 433 California Street, San Francisco, California 94104. 7. Owner: Jossey-Bass Inc., Publishers, 433 California Street, San Francisco, California 94104. 8. Known bondholders, mortgages, and other security holders owning or holding 1 percent or more of total amount of bonds, mortgages, or other securities: same as No. 7. 10. Extent and nature of circulation: (Note: first number indicates the average number of copies of each issue during the preceding twelve months; the second number indicates the actual number of copies published nearest to filing date.) A. Total number of copies printed (net press run): 2532, 2529. B. Paid circulation, 1) Sales through dealers and carriers, street vendors, and counter sales: 85, 40. 2) Mail subscriptions: 979, 919. C. Total paid circulation: 997, 959. D. Free distribution by mail, carrier, or other means (samples, complimentary, and other free copies): 125, 125. E. Total distribution (sum of C and D): 1122, 1084. F. Copies not distributed, 1) Office use, left over, unaccounted, spoiled after printing: 1410, 1445. 2) Returns from news agents: 0, 0. G. Total (sum of E, F1, and 2—should equal net press run shown in A): 2532, 2529.

I certify that the statements made by me above are correct and complete.

JOHN R. WARD
Vice-President